**THREE H**

*Cover design:* Dry-stone wall on Isaac Hall's Farm, High Studdon, Allendale (see pp. 2 & 3). *Photographed by Alan Taylor*

## DEDICATION

To the memory of
Christopher, my husband
and our fifty years together

For our family

# Three Hannahs

by

Hannah Henderson Taylor

William Sessions Limited
York, England

ISBN 1 85072 044 4

© Hannah H. Taylor 1989

Printed by
William Sessions Limited
The Ebor Press, York
England

# CONTENTS

*Page*

Maps: Friends' District Madagascar (1906)    viii
       Allendale and surrounding area    ix

Preface    x

CHAPTER ONE
     Hannah Hall Henderson    1
     1825-1910 *The First Hannah*

CHAPTER TWO
     Hannah Henderson Wilson    15
     1858-1945 *The Second Hannah*

CHAPTER THREE
     Emmeline Hannah Cadbury    57
     1883-1966 *The Third Hannah*

Bibliography    100

Index    101

Genealogies    106

# ILLUSTRATIONS

|  | Page |
|---|---|
| Preface | |
| Hannah Henderson with Hannah Henderson Cadbury | xi |

## CHAPTER ONE

| | |
|---|---|
| 'High Studdon' today *by Clare Norton from a photograph by Alan Taylor* | 3 |
| Mary Philipson, 1825 | 5 |
| Wedding certificate of Isaac Hall and Mary Philipson | 6 |
| Hannah and Matthew Henderson, c.1875 | 9 |
| The Kylie Cow *by Clare Norton* | 10 |
| Hannah Henderson driving her pony trap, c.1900, *by Clare Norton from a photograph* | 10 |
| Matthew Henderson, aged 80, on Alec's pony, c.1900, *by Clare Norton from a photograph* | 11 |
| Hannah Henderson, 1900, *from a portrait by Percy Bigland* | 13 |

## CHAPTER TWO

| | |
|---|---|
| William and Hannah Wilson before leaving for Madagascar in 1882 | 19 |
| Malagasy carrying chair *by Hannah H. Taylor from a photograph* | 23 |
| The Mission House *by Clare Norton from a photograph* | 25 |
| Village near the Mission House in Mandridrano *by Clare Norton from a photograph* | 27 |
| 'The Hope' today *by Clare Norton from a photograph by Alan Taylor* | 29 |
| Hannah Senior, c.1876, sister of William Wilson | 31 |
| The Three left in England in 1892 | 32 |

| | |
|---|---|
| William Wilson on Merrylegs *by Clare Norton from a photograph* | 39 |
| Broken pieces of Queen Ranavalona's crown | 42 |
| Hannah Wilson with Kenneth, 1899 | 46 |
| Queen Ranavalona in exile in Algeria | 49 |
| Queen Ranavalona's brooch *by Hannah H. Taylor from a photograph* | 50 |
| William and Hannah Wilson with Kenneth on their Silver Wedding day, 1907 | 53 |
| Hannah Wilson, c.1935 | 55 |

## CHAPTER THREE

| | |
|---|---|
| Emmie with her shady hat, Antananarivo, 1890 | 59 |
| Emma Cadbury, c.1876, sister of William Wilson | 65 |
| Emmie, 13-years old. *Portrait photograph* | 72 |
| Emmie, 1897 | 75 |
| Emmie at The Mount, 1898 | 76 |
| Engagement photographs of William Cadbury and Emmie, 1901 | 87 |
| Wast Hills, 1907 and c.1930 | 91 |
| Silver Wedding group of William and Emmeline, 1927 | 93 |
| Emmeline, County Commissioner, 1938 | 94 |
| William and Emmeline, c.1939 | 96 |
| Victorian candle holder from Emmeline's tree *by Hannah H. Taylor* | 97 |
| Oak leaf and oak fern *by Hannah H. Taylor* | 98 |
| Emmeline Hannah Cadbury, 1918, *a portrait by Charles M. Gere* | 99 |

vii

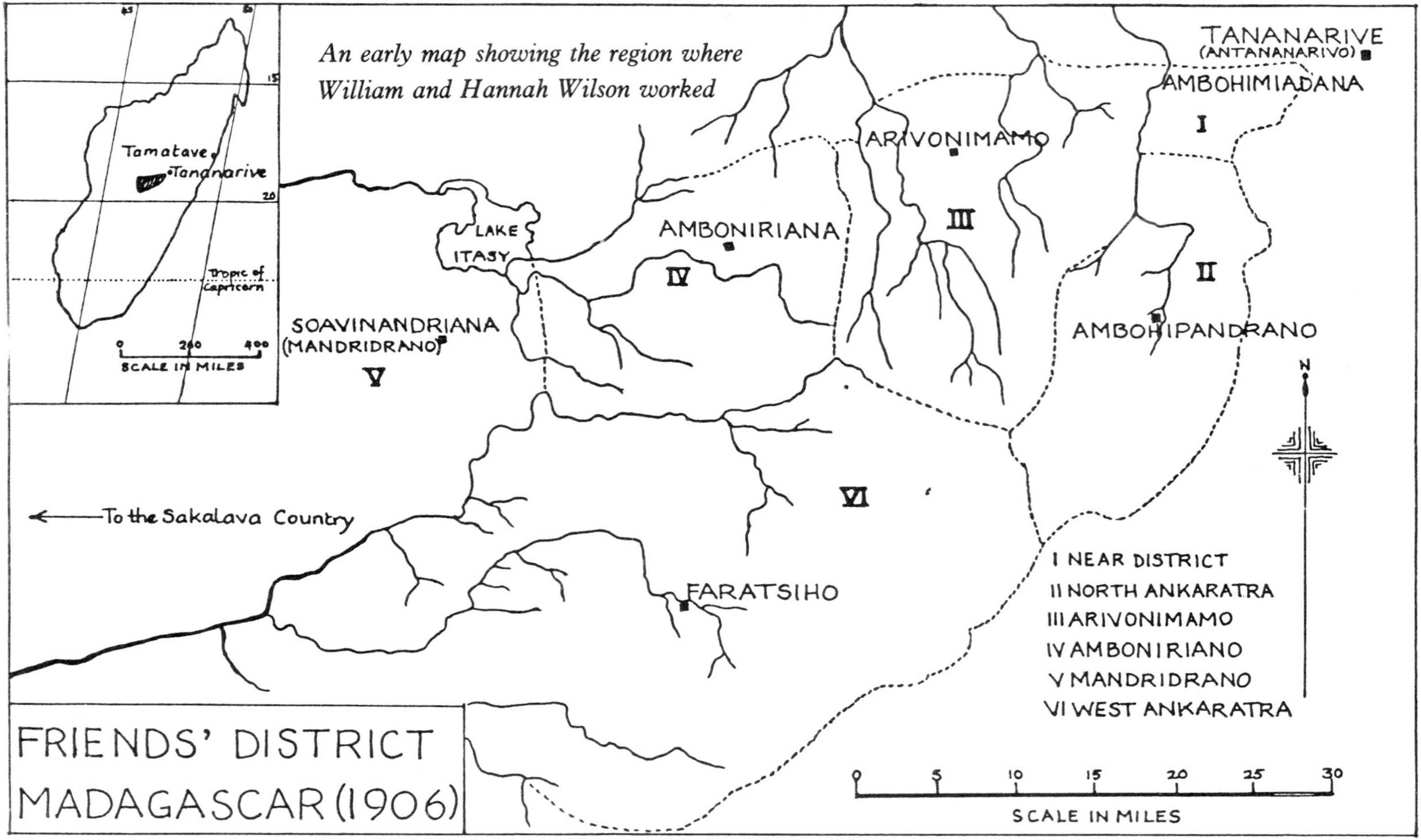

*An early map showing the region where William and Hannah Wilson worked*

I NEAR DISTRICT
II NORTH ANKARATRA
III ARIVONIMAMO
IV AMBONIRIANO
V MANDRIDRANO
VI WEST ANKARATRA

SCALE IN MILES
0  5  10  15  20  25  30

FRIENDS' DISTRICT
MADAGASCAR (1906)

Map of Allendale and surrounding area

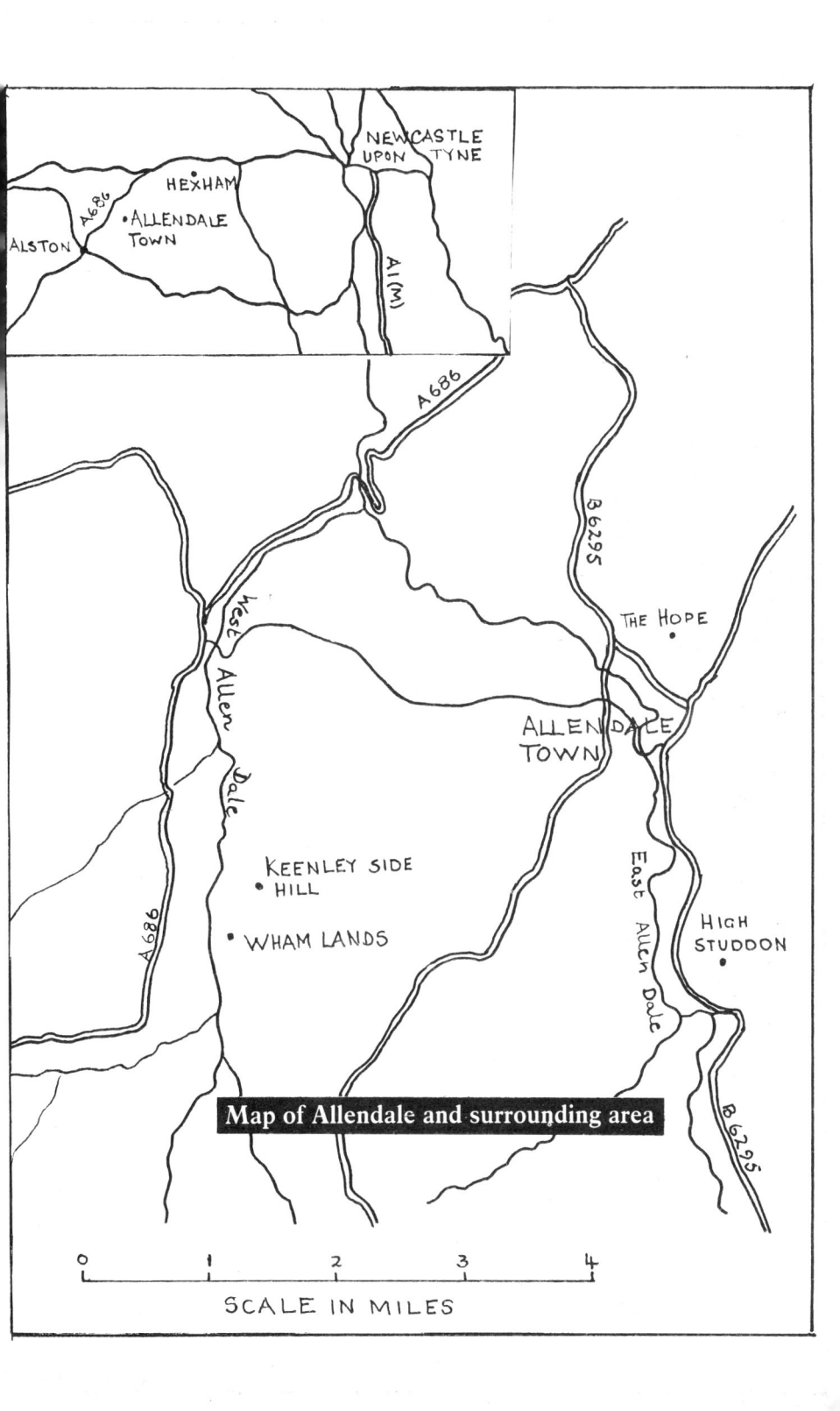

# PREFACE

WHEN I WAS TWO YEARS OLD my father and mother took me to see the great-grandmother Hannah Henderson, after whom I had been named. My mother would have liked to add Joyce to my name, and always called me Joy, but she was proud of the connection with her Allendale relations, and glad to show my father the place which held so many happy memories. The time must have been the early spring of 1906, and after a long train journey we arrived to find the Allendale town cab waiting for us, with clean straw on the floor to keep our feet warm. As we slowly climbed the hill to the home of my great-grandparents, I tried to look out at the dim countryside. It was the first time that I had ever been out in the dark, and this exciting drive was almost the only thing I remember about that very special visit.

It was this great-grandmother of mine who had told my mother the stories of her childhood, passed on so vividly that it seemed that they must be recorded. They form the background to the life of the first Hannah, together with some of the fascinating memories of her brother John Hall which were written for private circulation and given to me by his great-nephew Robert Wigham. From the time when my grandfather worked as a missionary in Madagascar letters became of vital importance and were read again and again, then kept as treasures. These letters are the basis of the other stories, without them I should never have known the details of life in Madagascar or of my mother's childhood and schooldays. There is inevitably some overlapping of the three lives, but told from different points of view they gain in interest.

I had many talks with my aunt and uncle, Mary Carroll and Alec Wilson of the story. Mary remembered Blackford and they both had happy memories of holidays in Allendale. My own family listened, criticised and helped with illustrations and photographs. Winifred White gave me valuable advice about details of life in Madagascar, and Margot Sessions made the book possible by her help and encouragement. To them all I am most grateful.

The brooch belonging to the Queen of Madagascar, and the small pieces of her crown form a part of the Wilson collection, to be presented to the Malagasy authorities in 1989.

October, 1988. Hannah H. Taylor

*Hannah Henderson Cadbury with Hannah Henderson, 1906*

CHAPTER I

# HANNAH HALL HENDERSON
# 1825 – 1910

## The First Hannah
Daughter of Isaac and Mary Hall
Married Matthew Henderson 1851

HANNAH HALL'S FOREBEARS CAME from the county of Northumberland. Many of the people of the border clans had Norse ancestry and Hall or Haal is a Norse name. They were small lairds and farmers, self reliant and independent, living up on the moors with their cattle during the summer months. Stern faced housewives would serve their menfolk with empty dishes if they thought that the time had come for another raid on English farms, and it was said that 'Those were most esteemed who in youth began to practise thefts and robberies.' Among them was Mad Jack Hall of family tradition, who followed Prince Charlie in '45 and is supposed to have ended his life on Tower Hill.

After the union of Scotland and England in 1707 the border slowly became more settled, though the Wardens of the Marches were to continue for some time. It was in 1652 and during George Fox's first visit to Northumberland, that many of the isolated communities had been drawn to Friends, and it is recorded that one officer declared 'You Quakers have done more to make the borders peaceable than I and my soldiers could do.' In spite of this persecution was severe. Hannah's grandmother was a Shield, and in 1660 five of her relations with eighteen others, all of Allendale, were taken at Meeting and carried to Hexham prison. In 1697 an early Isaac Hall was reported as exercising care for the relief of poor Friends of Berwick, Newcastle, and Hexham Meetings.

Hannah's father, another Isaac, a descendant of this Isaac Hall, was a farmer at a time when farms were still self-contained communities. Candles, rush lights and soap were made at home; peat for fuel was cut on the fells, and it was Hannah's mother's boast that all the winter long the spinning wheel was never silent. Mother and daughters took turns to sit and spin in a corner of the warm kitchen, and if they were busy, one of the maids would take up the task, while in the long evenings Isaac read aloud to them from *Barclay's Apology*, and *George Fox's Journal*. The wool was knitted into stockings, and it was usual in those days for the men on the farm to receive a homespun coat each year as part of their wages. Hannah's mother also spun the flax for linen sheets, two of which are still treasured in the family. Sheep and cattle were the mainstay of the farm, the hardier breeds of sheep feeding all summer with the cattle on the heather covered fells, though they were brought down in winter to more sheltered fields about the farm house. The blizzards of winter were a hazard and sheep might be caught and trapped under the drifts for days before they were found and dug out.

Isaac's farm, *High Studdon*, is still shown on maps of the district and lies two miles south of Allendale town. He was twenty-eight years old when his father died, and he continued to farm the land with the help of one man, John Graham. His eldest sister was married and his older brother had also left home, but two daughters remained to help his ageing mother. When Jeanie the second daughter married, Mary Philipson, a girl of sixteen, came to be a companion to the youngest daughter Sarah and to help with her share of the work.

Mary's father was a farmer and miner. In those days there were numerous small lead mines in the county worked by three or four men together and he seems to have been a partner in one of them.

Mary's mother came from a Quaker family but she had been disowned by her Meeting when it was known that her future husband was not a member of the Society of Friends, the usual practice in those days, when as they termed it, a member

*High Studdon today*

'married out'. She was a happy lively girl with dark hair and red cheeks who soon made friends with Sarah and became part of the family. It was a shock to Isaac's mother when gossiping neighbours began to remark that she was setting her cap at Isaac, and a severe scolding only made matters worse. Mary flew to Isaac begging him to say that this was not true. Isaac must have been a man of few words, but his half recognised feelings took shape as he looked at Mary's flushed cheeks and tearful eyes. All he said to her was 'Meet me at the fell gate tonight Mary, and bring thy cloak with thee,' but she knew what he meant. During that long and anxious day, Mary first took refuge with neighbours and then hid in a hay loft to escape her father who had arrived at *High Studdon* in a great state of indignation, both with his daughter and Isaac's mother. Isaac appeared quite unmoved, going stolidly about his work till the evening, then, mounting his horse, he rode away leaving one coat-tail in the hands of his distracted mother.

At the gate which led to the fells and the moor road Mary was waiting with John Graham, the farm man, on a stout horse. Isaac was determined to marry Mary, but decided that he could at least observe the proprieties which might soften the blow, so as they rode through the night, she sat pillion behind John. They reached Gretna Green next day and were safely united, Mary making her mark on the certificate drawn up by the blacksmith. John was dispatched to break the news, and Isaac, now with every right, took his wife up behind him to set out on a more leisurely journey home.

Once married Mary's welcome was never in doubt, though one of the inevitable consequences of the wedding was Isaac's disownment by Friends, though with characteristic persistence he continued to take Mary to Meeting. Mary's father was equally disturbed by the Gretna Green marriage and it was the Rector of Allendale, Isaac's old school master who, greatly concerned to regularise this hasty union, persuaded Isaac to let him marry them in church. Tradition has it that they were finally married in Meeting as well; it is certain that Mary applied for membership of the Society of Friends before many months had passed, and that they were both welcomed back into the Meeting, as well as into Isaac's home. She was to become a much beloved daughter and sister, and judging from an old silhouette and the angle at which she wore her newly acquired Quaker cap, she must have brought fresh life and gaiety into a sober household.

Her sister-in-law, Sarah, lived with the family to the end of her life helping to welcome and spoil Isaac and Mary's eleven children as they appeared. As the family grew a special room was added for her use, and from it she kept an eye on all that was going on. Though she liked to think herself delicate she was an ardent horsewoman, considering all other modes of travel unsafe, so that it is painful to record that she came to grief one day as she was setting out for Quarterly Meeting (the quarterly business meeting of Friends, organised on a county basis, which was also a social occasion much valued for exchanging news and views). She had a new outfit, dress, shawl and bonnet, and she was carried to the mounting block so that her shoes might not be soiled. The road from the farm was steep and rain

*Mary Philipson, 1825*

had made it slippery. Perhaps she was too absorbed in her new clothes to pick her way, for the horse in an unlucky moment came down and she was rolled in the mud. Poor Aunt Sarah, no one saw her at Quarterly Meeting that day, but she continued as the light of the family and her ways were lovingly remembered. She owned the first umbrella in Allendale, though her nephews declared that she always hid it during a shower to keep it dry. The doctor was paid £10 a year to visit her once a week and to keep her supplied with medicine, and it was a family joke that she sniffed at the bottles but never drank the contents.

    Mary must have been thankful for all Sarah's help and friendship as the family grew. She was a loving mother – singing to her babies and kissing them as she tucked them up in their cradles. She also loved law and order, and was the parent who disciplined them as they grew older.

Wedding Certificate of Isaac and Mary Hall, daughter of Francis Philipson (note blacksmith's spelling of Francis – Frances)

|  |  |
|---|---|
| No 122 For the Year of 1824 | These are to certify, to all Persons whom it may concern, that Isaac + Hall of Studdon and parish of Allendale County of Northumberland son of the late Isaac + of the aforesaid parish and county, and Mary Nattress of Studdon and parish of Allendale County of Northumberland Daughter of Frances Philipson of Knock Shield in the aforesaid parish and County came before me, and declared themselves to be both single Persons, and were lawfully married according to the Way of the Church of England, and agreeably to the Laws of Scotland. Given under my hand at SPRINGFIELD, near Gretna Green, this fifteenth day of October 1824  No 122, For the Year of 1824 |
| No 122 For the Year of 1824 | Before these Witnesses: Thomas Marshall Jane Rae           Isaac Hall                                        her                           Mary  +  Nattress                                       Mark |

She must have had great vitality and skill to manage a household where so much had to be done at home, and Hannah as her eldest daughter would soon feel proud to think that she was needed to help with the little brothers and sisters as they arrived. To feed such a family was a problem in itself and meals at *High Studdon* were plentiful but simple; all milk was skimmed and cream was used for butter which sold at 8d. a pound. As many as twenty cheeses were made each year, and there was cheese on the table at every meal. Breakfast for the children consisted of porridge with milk but no sugar, coffee and bread and butter, the bread being baked at home in great ten pound loaves from a mixture of wheat and rye flour. When staying with relations one might be given crowdy; this was a local substitute for porridge and was made by pouring boiling water onto toasted oatmeal; eaten with buttermilk the children thought it fit for a king. A leg of lamb was boiled for Sunday dinner and when it was finished everyone ate bacon for the main meal. There were dumplings and suet puddings with currants and raisins, and sometimes rice pudding. Tea was considered an extravagant meal – very strong freshly ground coffee with cream, and bread and butter, no hint here of the cakes and puddings of future generations.

Isaac too was an affectionate father; each day as he walked over the farm he liked to have some of the children with him, girls as well as boys. He never took a dog, going quietly among the sheep and cattle, counting them or moving them to fresh pasture. At one high point he could look out in all directions to the surrounding fells as they stretched away to Scotland and the Border heights, while to the east ran the valley that sheltered the head waters of the Tyne. From such a viewpoint men and women might have watched for the glint of sun on armour as the Roman cohorts marched northwards to join their comrades on the great wall; in Isaac's day four farm walls met there and gave shelter from any wind that blew; it was a good place to sit down on the grass with the children. There they would repeat Bible verses and poetry together or he would teach them the names of flowers and birds. Sometimes they gathered rushes for rushlights, or, taking an old horse would go up to the high fells to collect peat for the fire – the fuel mainly used on the farms in those days.

In 1835 when Hannah was ten years old a boarding school was opened at Wigton for the children of Friends. There was a local school which the Hall family had attended with the little Grahams, but at Wigton there was an opportunity for better education which was eagerly welcomed by Isaac, who sent all his children in turn. Hannah when she left became a nursery governess to a local family and spent some time in Newcastle, where she learnt to make pastry – a great accomplishment in her brothers' eyes. Four sisters stayed on at the school as pupil teachers; only Elizabeth and Jane returned home to help their mother until they married.

Isaac was a staunch supporter of the Society of Friends, and read all the early journals that he could find. He used the plain language and plain dress, while his wife and sister wore Quakerly muslin caps, even the bonnets of his little daughters were neatness itself. This did not spoil the excitement of Sunday when they were all packed into the farm cart to go to Meeting in Allendale; in earlier days Mary had ridden with a child behind her and a baby on her knee.

Did Isaac realise how much he depended upon Mary's love and support? Her little son John still young enough to be beside her with his sisters in Meeting (instead of on the men's side), sometimes wondered why there were tears on her cheeks as she sat in the gathered silence, her turbulent family quiet for a short hour. He was eleven years old when she died after an accident in 1853 and Susannah, her baby, was only two. Elizabeth and Jane were at home and could help Aunt Sarah to care for the little ones, but Isaac was desolate. He still remained the same affectionate father, but until his death eight years later, he seemed without any real interest in life.

Her mother had still been with them when in May 1851 Hannah left this loving home to marry Matthew Henderson, and live with him at *Wham Lands*, another farm in the beautiful Allendale Valley. Matthew's father Robert, who owned a farm in Allendale, had come south from Caithness at the time of the clearances, when numbers of crofters and small farmers were driven off the land and even deported, to make the great deer forests where sheep could be raised. Matthew was brought up as a Primitive Methodist, taught in Sunday School and was a

*Hannah and Matthew Henderson, c. 1875*

strict Sabbatarian. Though he never joined Friends he attended Meeting and was much in sympathy with the Society.

At *Wham Lands* Matthew and Hannah's ten children were born, another Hannah being fourth in the family. Sometime in the 70's there was a move to *Keenley Side Hill*, and in 1880 to *The Hope*, much nearer to Allendale town. Matthew was by now becoming an important member of the community, and it may be that this last move, to a farm on poorer land, was made so that he could be closer to his growing interests. He was a special constable, trustee and manager of the Savings Bank, an overseer of the parish and later chairman of the Parish Council, and at different times held other offices in the district. Hannah supported him in all his interests and, by her wise management of family affairs, left him free to pursue them; while he was the first to acknowledge the strength of her influence on his busy life.

In 1897 he retired from active farming to *Glenholme*, a tall grey house on the outskirts of the town, built for him by his daughter Lizzie. His son Matthew took over *The Hope*, but was persuaded to let his father have some land so that he might keep a cow or two and a few sheep and pigs, to provide the home-

*The Kylie Cow*

produced food which he preferred. It was a happy place for a child to visit, and his grandson Alec Wilson looked forward to his holidays there. There was a pony to ride and at one time a Kylie cow, a small Highland breed with a thick coat and long horns; she gave good milk, and Alec sometimes sat on her back as she was led from the byre. His daring sister Mary was not so lucky when she climbed onto the back of the little cow as she lay in the field. Badly startled she lurched to her feet and set off at a gallop; Mary clung desperately to the thick hair, but after a few moments fell off onto the grass. She counted those moments as a triumph and could say indignantly at the age of ninety '*I* was the one who rode the Kylie cow!'

*Hannah Henderson driving her pony trap c.1890*

*Matthew, aged 80, riding Alec's pony*

Matthew had always been attracted by unusual breeds. Among the sheep there was a Border Leicester tup to be evaded, a belligerent animal, which on one occasion even knocked down Matthew himself. Alec felt proud when his grandfather, now over eighty, rode his pony Angus, and like all the grand-children he delighted in following Aunt Fanny, collecting the warm eggs for her as she went the rounds of the poultry house.

Hannah remained in the background, dominated by her three unmarried daughters, Fanny, Amy and Maggie. We can imagine her driving in the pony-trap to Meeting, or over the moors to visit some of her many relations, or sitting at home in her straight-backed chair with her knitting in her hands. She was still the bee-keeper of the family; when they swarmed, she would go out and fearlessly hive them with her bare hands, though Matthew was certain to be stung if he so much as came to the door to watch her. She was often silent, but with time to listen to a perceptive little grand-daughter, and to talk to her of the days when she herself was a child.

Towards the end of her life her portrait was painted by the Quaker artist Percy Bigland. He insisted on her wearing her soft silk wedding shawl with its worn fringe; her lace collar was replaced by a wisp of white chiffon fastened by her only piece of jewelry, the cornelian brooch which had been Matthew's silver wedding gift. The painting shows her sitting upright in the wooden armchair which was her most comfortable seat and she looked so life-like, that Matthew, coming into the room where the unfinished picture was still on its easel, said in surprise, 'Thou art up very early this morning.'

Her daughters were outraged by the artist's change of her costume, especially by the ragged fringe of the shawl, which was painted with unnecessary realism, but Hannah still sits with the light on her silver hair, serene in the faith of a long life and with a smile in her eyes for the younger generation and their pre-occupation with the unessentials which matter so little in the end.

Visiting friends and relations delighted to see the peaceful happiness of these last years spent together. Matthew died in the winter of 1908, and Hannah only lived two years without him. They were laid to rest in the Burial Ground of the small Allendale Meeting House. Halls, Shields and Hendersons are there, for the Meeting, once a centre of Quakerism in Northumberland, was largely supported by a wide group of cousins. Even today one of their descendants may find that they are related, not only to some who meet there each Sunday, but to almost all of those who lie so peacefully under the grass outside.

*Hannah Henderson – a portrait by Percy Bigland, R.A., 1900*

CHAPTER II

# HANNAH HENDERSON WILSON
# 1858 – 1945

## The Second Hannah
Daughter of Hannah and Matthew Henderson
Married William Wilson 1882

HANNAH'S PARENTS MATTHEW AND HANNAH HENDERSON lived at the farm of *Wham Lands* above Allen Head for the first 20 years of their married life. Two daughters were born, and a son who only lived three and a half years. Then came Hannah who was to be the leader of the younger half of the family.

Four more girls followed Hannah, with twin boys who were so alike that very few people could tell them apart. One was named for his father Matthew, and the other was called Robert for the little brother who had died. One day their mother found them standing on a chair in front of her mirror, and heard Matthew say, 'You get down Robbie and then I shall know which is me.' They puzzled their younger relations to the end of their days.

One picture remains of the earliest years: Hannah burnt her finger; we were not told how she did it, but she was certainly disobeying her mother when it happened, and when she expected to be comforted she received a sharp scolding and no sympathy at all. This was more than the little girl could bear, and with the smarting finger held in a cup of cold water to relieve the pain, she ran to their neighbour, a childless woman, who was always ready to welcome the *Wham Lands* family, and who was little Hannah's special friend.

As the family grew, Hannah, active and daring, invented games for the younger children and often led them into scrapes. At a later home, *Keenley Side Hill*, there was a long wall beside a sloping lane on the top of which they ran, finally catching at the branch of a tree to swing themselves off onto the grass. Ponies and dogs were their playmates, and they loved one small shetland, Dinah, which Hannah used to lead through the house when her mother was safely out of the way. She once tried to take it upstairs and perhaps it was fortunate that at this point the pony, for once, had a mind of its own, and refused to climb the staircase.

Not far from *Wham Lands* there lived an elderly man named John Henderson; he was not related to Matthew, and kept very much to himself, being known in the neighbourhood as 'the miser': he was another of young Hannah's friends, and she liked to ride over to visit him, often returning with the present of a sixpence. One day she came home in a temper declaring that after all John Henderson was a miser for he had given her a bad yellow sixpence; she had never possessed a half sovereign, and it is to be hoped that she forgave her old friend. The yellow sixpence became a family joke.

The children lived active country lives, governed by the strict religious habits of their parents. Meeting-going was still an event, and Hannah's mother like her grandmother, rode with a child before and behind her in the early days. The little girls were deeply impressed by Victorian ideas of propriety in matters of dress and behaviour. Their mother was of a generation of Quakers who wore no wedding ring, and it was her daughters who, at the time of her silver wedding insisted that she must have one and so become respectable. They rode their hardy fell ponies, and as they had no side-saddles, sometimes pulled the off-side stirrup across the saddle, balancing precariously with both stirrups on one side so that they might look like ladies. One sheep-shearing day the meat was short and Hannah was sent into Allendale to fetch an extra leg of mutton. Carrying it on her knee she set off for home, to be over-taken by the doctor, who, as he came up, touched her pony into a canter; on the broad grassy edge of the road she could manage well enough, but when they came to the farm gate the doctor, with a flourish of his whip and a cheerful 'good-bye' went on, leaving her with the heavy joint of meat, an excited pony, and the gate to open and close behind her. She never forgave him for the slight to her youthful dignity. 'I did not mind him making me canter with him,' she told her grandaughter many years later, 'but no gentleman would have left me as he did without stopping to open the gate.'

In 1871, when she was thirteen years old, Hannah joined her older sisters at Wigton School; she stayed there as a pupil until April 1875 when she became a pupil teacher. A young man, William Wilson, joined the teaching staff in May that year. His elder sister Emma had married Richard Cadbury of Birmingham as his second wife, and through this Quaker connection William had already spent two years at the Flounders Institute, a teacher training college at Ackworth.

He was only at Wigton for one year, but he gave Hannah his first little present on her seventeenth birthday, and she had her photograph taken especially for him. It shows the black wavy hair and the dark eyes inherited from her mother, but she looks altogether too serious for the lively girl who attracted William's out-going nature.

From Wigton William went on to widen his experience of teaching, and in 1876 became a master at Waterford Friends' School in Ireland. There he joined the Society of Friends and in that year, when he was only nineteen, he was accepted by the Friends Foreign Mission Association for service in Madagascar, a long-held ambition which first took hold of him when, as a child of seven, he heard of the persecution of Malagasy Christians under their cruel Queen Ranavalona I. After her death the persecution ceased and several missionary associations answered the call of the new Christian queen for help in rebuilding the scattered church. William landed in the island in September 1877, on the eve of his twentieth birthday. Hannah, with whom he had shared all his hopes, stayed at home growing and learning, and writing him the long epistles for which she always apologised. 'I am sorry to send thee such a shabby letter,' she says, more than once, as she finishes several pages.

In January 1878 Hannah left Wigton to spend a year at The Mount School, York. This move may have been suggested by Wigton, who kept her on their list of teachers, but wanted her to have further education in a higher form. Of all her family she was the only one to follow her Aunt Margaret Hall to York. Uniform was still strictly plain though the girls might wear white collars on their afternoon dresses if they embroidered them themselves. Bonnets had to be worn, but Hannah had one which became a hat in the holidays (the bonnet lockers were still there in her granddaughter's day, but by then hats were allowed if simply trimmed without flowers or feathers). Large shawls for use in the garden hung in long folds from the pegs in the cloakroom, and there the girls used to sit, in the 'muffled separation' described in a school song, while they desperately revised for their examinations. One other remembrance was of a girl who always got into bed fully dressed to save time in the morning!

Hannah returned to Wigton in January 1879 for one more year as a teacher, then she went home to help her mother until the time came for William to carry her off to Madagascar.

It seems strange that William had been sent to such a far away country without any preparation, but there were already eight Quaker missionaries in the field to help and advise him, as well as members of the London Missionary Society with whom they worked for the Protestant Churches.

William flung himself into everything that was going, from the teaching, which was his special responsibility, to the mixing of Gregory powders for a medically minded colleague, but first and foremost was his determination to master the language.

His work was chiefly in the capital Antananarivo, but as his knowledge of Malagasy improved he was sent on short expeditions into the country to preach and teach in the Sunday Schools, and after a year was given the care of a large district. Wherever he went he saw the need for medical help and became firmly convinced that every missionary should possess some knowledge of medicine. When he was recalled for his first furlough in 1880 he registered and qualified as a medical student at the London Hospital, but after a year the call to go

*William and Hannah Wilson before leaving for Madagascar in 1882*

back to Madagascar became urgent for there was so much work to be done. So he gave up his training, and this time Hannah was waiting to go with him. They were married in 1882 and set out at once on the long journey – a fellow missionary Clara Herbert going with them.

They landed just in time to escape the bombardment of the coast by the French navy, which was at that time giving 'protection' to the outlying tribes, who were rebelling against the domination of the central government of the Hova tribe. The only immediate effect on life in Antananarivo, standing high on the plateau in the centre of the island, was that mails became very uncertain, so that sometimes letters were delayed for up to nine months.

Once there they were warmly welcomed, and a small house was eventually found for them. Oil lamps, earth closets and a lack of plumbing generally were no great surprise to Hannah. They were still accepted in the country at home, as was the easy supply of domestic help. It was harder to keep up the standard of appearance that had been expected by her mother and sisters, but mission wives struggled bravely, with little modification of the voluminous dress of the day. Hats of course were always worn, but in the capital gloves, flounces, parasols and scarves came out for garden parties, and no one would have thought of being seen without stockings at any time. Hannah entered into it all, getting to know the wives and children of the missionary community, learning the language, playing energetic tennis, helping at tea parties and endearing herself to everyone. Wives at that time were not counted as missionaries, but they lived full and active lives, supporting their husbands and each other, and upholding, as well as trying to teach, the home standards that they felt to be such an important part of their witness.

During that first year, in spite of the friendship of this busy English community Hannah often felt lonely. William was occupied all day, and was away in his district each month, sometimes for as much as a fortnight at a time. Even in England many young wives of her generation felt lost during the early days of married life, with servants to do the work of the house, and a part-time job unthinkable; in addition Hannah was in a strange land amongst strangers.

What a welcome must have been waiting for William each night, and how happy and satisfying the times they spent together, as he told her about his adventures and plans. Joy in the work and in each other was the deep foundation of their life and it was recognised by everyone who met them.

In July of 1883 Emmeline Hannah was born and her mother, Hannah, was never to be lonely again. She had spent much time in making the first small garments for this eagerly awaited baby. There were no elaborate frills or delicate laces, but every fine seam was stitched with love and hope, and the little gowns and nightdresses were as beautiful as tucking and feather stitching could make them. Now she had an absorbing interest which helped to pass the days she spent by herself with her baby when William was away. When he was working in the capital he would hurry home in the evenings determined to take his share as a father, amazing Hannah by his deft handling of such a scrap of a daughter.

It was a friendly world for a child; the brown face and smiling dark eyes of her dear nurse Neney and her father's Malagasy friends in their white lambas were as familiar to her as the members of the large European missionary community. The Society of Friends at this time chiefly worked with the London Missionary Society and shared the development of the Protestant churches in the centre of the island, husbands and wives of both churches supporting each other and making close friendships.

In 1885 a brother Ashlin came to join Emmie, but with the joy of a son there came constant anxieties for his mother. It is difficult now to realise the dread of tropical diseases, particularly the recurring malaria which was so little understood, and though there were no snakes in the town garden there were other perils for the children. One night both parents were horrified to see a large scorpion on the blanket which covered the sleeping baby. They hardly dared to breath lest child or insect made a fatal move. William tiptoed out of the room and returned with a fountain-pen filler full of chloroform, from which he let a drop fall on the scorpion's head, when to his intense relief it collapsed.

In spite of all his mother's care the little boy was not as strong as Emmie, and when in the cold weather he developed fever, it was followed by bronchitis. A qualified doctor was working with the London Missionary Society at that time, but in spite of his devoted help little Ashlin died. Emmie, young as she was, realised something of her parents' loss as her father put her into Hannah's arms that night. Hannah never forgot the sudden bereavement, and when another daughter Lucy Mary was born it almost seemed that she resented her for taking the place of this beloved first son.

However, there were now two little daughters to plan for and Hannah comforted her sore heart by working over frocks and pinafores, until her husband feared for her health.

Soon afterwards they moved to Mandridrano, William's district in the grass covered cattle country. How he had loved planning their home-to-be. The building called up all his invention and skill, but at last it proved to be all he wanted. His especial pride was the construction of a bullock cart for bringing stones and bricks to the site, instead of employing men to carry them. He often lamented his ignorance of common things, and wished that he had learnt more about them – now he had to work out his problems as they came.

The house was built of wood and laterite, the red earth which hardens after it is cut into blocks. The roof was thatched with grass, and there was a wide veranda running round the ground floor. The chimneys and the pillars supporting the upper floors were of bricks, and when at last it was ready, the family, with servants and bearers, set off on the three day journey from the capital. Hannah and the children rode in palanquins (the Malagasy word is filanjana) – seats slung on poles and carried by four men. William on his pony went to and fro, showing the way and cheering and encouraging them all.

They were warmly welcomed by the people of Mandridrano who were already William's friends, and who brought the customary generous presents of rice, eggs, chickens and turkeys. As soon as they were fairly settled they gave the expected house warming party. There was a magic lantern show in the school-room with hymn singing and prayers. As the guests left they were all given fruit and currant buns, for which Hannah had used some of her precious store of flour. These buns were greeted as a great novelty and the few currants were the last wonder of the day – some, indeed, were sure that they must be flies and would not eat them.

Wherever he went William planted a garden, and in time they had vegetables and fruit of their own, for food in

Madagascar was monotonous. Flour and other expensive extras had to be imported, and meat was not always easy to get. At one time they were eating the everlasting rice with chicken three times a day. Milk was another problem, but William was determined to tame the local cattle and eventually succeeded.

*Malagasy carrying chair, the fifth man relieves the others*

Isolated on a country station difficulties seemed doubled. Parcels from home were eagerly looked for, not only for the little presents and luxuries that they contained, but for the necessary children's shoes, and the materials, buttons, and cottons for dress-making, as well as medicines and reading matter. Hannah had taken with her a small sewing machine and made her own and the children's clothes, even finding time to run up dresses for her friends, no small task when a 'print' for morning wear took six yards of material. She loved her children to look spruce and prim, as their father said, and spent hours on her sewing. In the dry weather the red earth of the country turned to dust which clung to everything it touched, and even rubbed off the walls of the houses, so Hannah was fortunate in having plenty of help with her washing. The washerman went with them on their first holiday so that William as well as his little daughter could have fresh white clothes each day. He was paid 6/8d. a month, and would of course have his food and accommodation. Even on missionary pay this was not considered unduly extravagant, as he washed all the servants' clothes as well.

It comes as a surprise to find that slaves were generally employed even in missionary families. Hannah wrote home in 1889 to explain William's plan of helping to free the people who worked for him. She tells of an old woman, Ratasy, who was a slave when she first came as a nurse for Mary, and who then possessed only one garment; and continues:—

> She earns 5/-d. a month wages, but 4/-d. of that goes every month to pay for her freedom. Ratasy is quite free now, but she had to pay £16. for her freedom. We advance the money and they pay it back at the rate of 4/-d. a month. Of course we give them help, but still find it much better to let them work off the money; they are more grateful. In some cases where they have been given their freedom they have gone, and with their first money bought a slave for themselves. We have helped to free ten slaves, and believe that each case has turned out quite satisfactorily. Half our servants are free, and half are still slaves. I keep all the money of the latter half and see that they do not waste it. Two of them, who are still boys, have quite a nice sum in my keeping.

*Mission House in Mandridrano*

William and Hannah took the system as they found it, and tried to make it work as fairly as they could. There was some sharp criticism from visitors to the island of missionaries who kept slaves, but it was not till the French occupation in 1895 that slavery was officially abolished.

William had only had one year's medical training, and was not a qualified doctor, but he had prepared as much as was possible to help the sick, and wherever he went the Malagasy flocked to him for help. When smallpox threatened in the capital he sent home for serum, and vaccinated Emmeline with the only phial that had survived the journey; other children needed help, so he successfully used the pus from her arm to protect them until it finally dried up and the wound healed. He also studied dentistry for a short time while in England and had a reputation for pulling teeth.

In Mandridrano something had to be done for the people who arrived to see him, and he built a number of cottages to shelter them, so that when whole families arrived with a sick relation they could stay with the invalid and feel more at home. In this way he laid the foundation of a small hospital. Hannah entered into the work by helping to provide suitable food, caring for the babies, and rejoicing over William's remarkable successes, but she confessed that she dreaded the invasions which sometimes spread into their own house making the work almost intolerable. Whatever happened no one was turned away without some help and comfort, and little Emmeline wondered at the happy look on her parents' faces as they made room for yet another patient and his family. The district's bad reputation for fever made skilled help difficult to get, but they were greatly cheered and supported by kind and loving letters from personal friends at home who sent special gifts of money to help with the work, though this was not popular with the mission treasurer, who understandably felt that funds should be held in common.

From Emmeline's account of these years it was a happy time for her. Baby Mary was a joy to them all. Hannah reports that 'She is very very fat, not too fat, but she is very comfortable.' William thought her winning and charming; he says 'Her merry little voice and romping rings through the house.' Hannah was more anxious for Emmie who seemed to them so lonely, with only her baby sister as a companion. Even William's patience was tried as she persisted in following him about, but Emmie adored her father, and it seems likely that she preferred his company to that of anyone else, and saw no reason for playmates when he was near.

For Hannah the isolation closed down. As time passed she was more often under the weather, taking longer to recover from fever and with little energy. Perhaps the worst anxiety was the recurring malaria from which there seemed no escape. Even William's buoyant spirits were affected by his own attacks, and more so by the sufferings of Hannah and the children. Also when illness came the hostile elements among the local people around them pressed closer, and the witch doctors grew bolder.

William continued his journeys to the scattered congregations, and sometimes rode beyond their boundaries, for, with other missionaries, he was urged by the Christian Queen to push further into the wild Sakalava country on their

*Village near the Mission House in Mandridrano*

doorstep, in order to evangelise the tribes which were opposed to the central government. Hannah, left alone with the children and their devoted servants, would climb the hill behind the house to look out over the grass-covered landscape and wonder where William was riding; at least once during the time at Mandridrano the horizon was alight with burning villages and who knew how soon the raiders might reach the mission. With her adventurous spirit and dedication to the work she must have driven herself to the limit, reaching out to the needs around her and still creating with William the warm loving home which little Emmeline remembered all her life, but it is not surprising that by September of 1889 Hannah was seriously ill and that William, under the combined strain of being husband, doctor and nurse sent an urgent request for help to Antananarivo. Writing to his mother he said 'There is no one near with whom to take counsel. What it would be without the dear Lord to fly to in our time of need I dare not think.'

The nearest mission station was forty-five miles away, and from there a fresh messenger went on to the capital. Dr. Fenn of the London Missionary Society set out as soon as the news came through, but it was not until the following day, fifty hours after the message had been sent, that he arrived at Mandridrano. He found Hannah improving, though prostrate with extreme nervous exhaustion, but with his help and encouragement she managed to face life again. Her beautiful black hair was already nearly white. Her recovery was slow, and when a parcel arrived from home, usually such a store of help and pleasure, she wrote an understandably exasperated letter to her sister Lizzie:–

> Thank thee for the parcel. The hats are very pretty – More about them another time, but however did thou come to forget Emmie's shoes or boots. She is so badly off she is out at the toes and really has nothing to wear, so send me two or three pairs as soon as thou can – say one pair of tens and two pairs of elevens. Excuse more, I am so tired that I cannot write more . . .

To this letter William added a note:–

> I am sorry to say Hannah is knocked up again after her struggles with Baby and no power on earth could have stopped her.

In the following May the whole family were again suffering from malaria, and as Hannah was pregnant they moved to the capital, Antananarivo, for a rest and change. This proved to be a change for the better but no rest, for as Hannah said, 'They were so feasted and run after.' William proudly wrote home:–

> You see mother, a man may be liked and respected and his friends glad to see him, but it is the wife with her thorough genuineness who wins her way into every corner of folks' hearts – it was extremely pleasing to see the evident pleasure it was to most to see dear Hannah and the two little girls.

Later that month Hannah and the children went with Mrs. Johnson, another missionary wife who was also suffering from fever, to stay in a holiday home at Isoavina where they had a real rest; reading, sewing, and teaching the children in the peace of the country.

They did not return to Mandridrano though William continued to oversee the district, and undertook further long journeys. In August of 1890 another son William Alexander was born, and in September they sailed for home.

*The Hope, Allendale, today*

On their return to England the whole family went to stay at *The Hope* in Allendale with Hannah's parents. They found the winds cold, but the good air of the hills and the active life on the farm were just what they needed to help them to recover their health after the long years of heat and fever, as well as the overwork in Mandridrano. William was especially warmed by the loving welcome of the whole family. Matthew Henderson did not say much but he delighted in the children and his eyes were always on them as they laughed and played with their cousins and many aunts.

Names in the Wilson and Henderson families are confusing, Emmas and Hannahs following each other till it is difficult to disentangle them; to add to the confusion baby Mary of Madagascar now became Lucy and remained so until after her father's death.

During this time in Allendale Hannah, the mother, became a girl again as she introduced the delights of her country childhood to her little daughters. The pony-trap drives over the hills to visit relations were in themselves a new experience for the children as there was still very little wheeled transport in Madagascar. The harvest was almost over when they arrived but blackberries and nuts still ripened in the lanes; there were hens to be watched and their hidden nests discovered. Perhaps one of the special joys was the gathering of the mushrooms which appeared so mysteriously in the grass, their cool white caps lined with pleated pink. One morning Hannah and the children found a new crop growing in the field where the bull was turned out; running to the opposite end of the field Hannah deposited Lucy on top of the wall, telling her to make as much noise as possible; then, while the bull was being distracted, she climbed nimbly over at the other end to pick her mushrooms.

William would join the cousins when they walked over the fells with their guns. There were many grouse in those days and in the early morning the blackcock came down to feed on the stooked corn in the fields near the farm.

Christmas was spent in Birmingham with Richard and Emma Cadbury (William's sister and her husband) and here they found another large family to welcome them. Richard Cadbury had for some years been interested in William's career and had given him help and encouragement; now there were further possibilities to be discussed with this wise friend and brother-in-law.

Although William had once given up medical studies, the quiet time among the hills of Northumberland now confirmed his deep concern to qualify as a doctor before returning to Madagascar. This meant a training of about four years but would lead, he believed, to his special contribution to the work of the mission. So a house was found in London where Hannah could make a home for the children and William returned as a student to the London Hospital. During 1891 he took his first medical examinations. He found the work exacting and hated being cooped up, as he said, in a city, but he looked forward to the experiences of the next two years, and there were times of escape to Allendale, with long days spent in the wide spaces of the open fells.

Towards the end of 1891 Hannah knew that another baby was on the way and that four children in their small London house would be more than she could manage, so the sad pattern of a divided family began. All over England at this time there were children living with relatives while their parents were overseas; sometimes, with no home to go to, they stayed all the year round at boarding schools. There were no exciting holiday flights to bring the families together and the uncertain mail services added to the sense of separation. Many found kind homes with uncles and aunts and it was William's eldest sister, another Hannah, who offered to take Emmie, now nine years old, as a companion for her daughter Dorothy who was about the same age. Her husband Charles Senior was vicar of the parish of Blackford just north of Carlisle. In anticipation of the inevitable parting when her parents returned to Madagascar, it seemed kindest to settle the child at once in a family where she could hope to stay and where her education with Dorothy could continue without interuption.

*Hannah Senior c.1876,
sister of Emma Cadbury and William Wilson*

*The Three left in England:*
*Emmie (holding Basil), Mary and Alec*

In June 1892 Samuel Basil was born and later in the summer the whole family were re-united in Allendale, Emmie delighted to see her baby brother for the first time and to be with her father and mother again. Eighteen months later William took his M.R.C.S. and L.R.C.P. degrees, and, now as a fully qualified doctor, could return to Madagascar and the work he loved.

There was no question of their taking the older children with them. Alec, only four years old, went to his Aunt Emma in Birmingham. Her three eldest daughters were already grown up, and her youngest, Beatrice, was almost too old for the nursery, but Emma Denham, her nurse, still ruled there. It was a haven of warmth and comfort for any of the family in search of peace and sympathy, and Alec at four years old needed just the care which she could give to him, and, while filling the place of a little brother, would bring the tall nursery rocking horse to life again. Lucy was to have joined Emmie at Blackford, but Hannah Senior (William's sister), a greatly beloved aunt, was far from strong and as she had a family of grown up stepchildren, as well as a son and daughter of her own, she now felt that the care of two additional small girls was more than she could undertake: so for this reason Lucy aged seven went to her in Emmie's place and Emmie was welcomed into the family of Joseph Firth Clark of Doncaster, where another little daughter was waiting to be her friend. One can almost hear the concern of the Madagascar Committee as the Wilson children were discussed and the relief when this kind offer was made; it proved to be a very happy arrangement.

Hannah was heart-broken at the thought of leaving her three and clung to Basil as her only comfort. He was a beautiful little boy and the voyage went well, but on the journey to the capital he developed fever and dysentry and two days before Christmas 1894 he died, leaving William and Hannah doubly desolate as they thought of the other children so far away. For Emmie at least it was a continuing grief, and two years later, when she was thirteen, she wrote lovingly to her mother at Christmas time, 'We shall all think of dear little Basil on the 23rd. but he is quite happy now and I dare say he will spend his Christmas rejoicing in heaven with the angels, won't he mother dear.'

Hannah herself had been very ill with a high fever but she bravely took up life again knowing how much William needed her. He had now been put in charge of the English Hospital, situated at the foot of the great hill on which Antananarivo was built; it was about forty minutes' ride away from the centre of the city. William and Hannah were given a house adjoining the main building, and set about planting yet another garden. One of Hannah's first parties was for the twenty-four Malagasy medical students who were William's special care. She gave them a meal of goose with green vegetables, beef with tomatoes, and curried duck, all served with rice, and followed up this substantial first course with tinned peaches and pineapple and custard, bread and butter, cake, jam tarts, jelly and tea. The guests came at 5.30 and stayed till 9 o'clock, enjoying much talk, music and bagatelle before they all joined together in a family prayer and then departed. Food must have been plentiful at this time despite the threatenings of war with France, and Hannah's tradition of English North-country hospitality must have delighted her visitors.

She continued to grieve for Basil, but comforted herself in visiting the hospital and taking a warm interest in the children there. She led a busy life for she was never without visitors in the house, and sometimes they came with fever, or in such an exhausted condition that it took weeks to nurse them back to health. It says much for her powers of organisation that she could do this successfully while entertaining daily callers, who loved to stay and talk in the friendly Malagasy way. Being a farmer's daughter she evidently looked on William's dogs, sometimes five or more at once, as a pleasant distraction, adding a cat of her own and rejoicing in frequent families of kittens. She also found time to take up her Malagasy lessons, and to teach sewing to a class of sixty-five little girls, collecting the infrequent sweets that came her way, until she had enough for them all. Hannah, of course, had servants to help her and some at this time were still slaves, but they, too, needed her care, and the planning and oversight of their work.

Social activities, picnics and tennis parties were greatly enjoyed. One old photograph shows several Malagasy girls clutching tennis rackets so they must have been introduced to this new form of amusement. The missionaries themselves attended royal occasions at the Palace, but their wives were not forgotten and were invited to tea parties and picnics in the Palace garden where they learnt to know and admire their hostess Queen Ranavalona III.

For some years previously William, as Secretary of the self-appointed British Committee of Safety, had realised that there was a threat of a French invasion and had written to the English Foreign Minister, Sir Edward Grey. In the early months of 1895 the French landed in strength and began making their way inland. Even at this stage the Malagasy of the capital found it hard to believe that they were seriously threatened, but many Europeans left or sent away their wives and children, so that in September of that year the missionary community was comparatively small. It had been arranged that should the capital be attacked, they would take refuge in the compound of the new English Hospital which was built on level ground at some distance from the city, facing the steep rise on the summit of which stood the Queen's palace; behind it rose one of the rolling hills which form the central plateau of the island.

In October Hannah wrote of their experiences during the next weeks in a letter to William's sister Emma:–

My dear Emma,

You are certain to see an account in the papers of the taking of Antananarivo but I must give you a little of our experience last Monday.

We were for five hours in the very thick of the fight and could not have chosen a more prominent position if we had tried. Shells went whizzing over our heads (three bursting in the grounds) and bullets were flying in all directions. The hospital and all the outbuildings were crowded with natives and yet nobody was hurt.

On the Thursday (Sept. 26th.) all the members of our mission in the capital with the exception of Mr. Clark, came over to our house to stay and nine members of the L.M.S. took refuge in the large hospital and five of the S.P.G. made their home in the infectious hospital.

On the Thursday morning the people were in a great state of jubilation as a report reached town that the whole French army had been annihilated; we did not believe the story but the natives did and rushed up to the Palace to congratulate the Queen; by night their spirits had fallen below zero as it was evident that the French were very near, about eight miles to the west of the capital; on Friday they went north toward the old capital (Ambahimanga) and on Saturday came towards town again. On Sunday afternoon we went up a hill just at the back of us and with our glasses watched the French marching along the hills opposite to us. The Malagasy were firing away at them but all to no purpose for they were quite out of range. Sunday night we slept very well, knowing that the French would not come on any further before morning, and directly after breakfast we went on to the hill again and saw them coming down the hills very rapidly, and as the Malagasy had planted a cannon on the top of the hill we were on and had commenced firing, we thought it was time we were making our way home, and just as we reached the house a shell came whizzing over our heads and two or three minutes after one fell in the compound between our house and Miss Byam's, part of the shell falling on the roof of Miss Byam's house. [Miss Byam was the lady superintendent.] The next shell fell within a few yards of the infectious hospital. It was an anxious time until the French silenced the cannon behind us and the natives ran away with it. We thought all danger for us was over but presently the whole hillside was alive with Malagasy soldiers; some few came into the compound but when asked to retire they did so at once and, after some brisk firing on both sides and considerable shelling, the Malagasy all ran away and the French appeared on the top of the hill and we had about an hour's quietness. I was so tired that I went to lie down but I could not rest and did not care to be alone, for we were in great danger from the Malagasy battery opposite to us; we were in the line of fire and did not feel sure of their aim. The French however pretty quickly silenced that battery and bent their energies on the Palace. We watched the shells falling in all directions but it was not until three had fallen and done considerable damage in the Palace yard that the Hova pulled down their flag at 3.27 p.m. saving themselves from utter destruction by three minutes, for the French had their cannon loaded with memalile shells which were to be fired at 3.30 p.m. and one of which would have been sufficient to destroy half the town, especially as the Malagasy had *50,000* barrels of gun powder in the large Palace. (This of couse we have been told since.) By 6 p.m. we were inundated with French wounded and sick; that first night between 50 and 60 came in, since then the numbers have reached over 100 and still they keep coming, but they generally have two or three deaths each day.

I have been to town for the first time to-day; it does not look very different but it seems strange to see so many Europeans walking about the roads. The French have brought such numbers of mules with them, poor patient creatures, I don't know how they live for this is the very worst time of the year for grass. The men look so tired and thin – ditto the horses. We had our first thunder storm and rain yesterday but we cannot expect any more for another month.

There are 10 sick or wounded officers in the big hospital; Miss Byam has food to prepare for them. I have bread made every other night. The Malagasy nurses have been very good but it must have been a trial to them to have to set to work to nurse their enemies all at once and having no choice in the matter. I sometimes feel that we are only now at the beginning of our troubles; the French have settled down here taking two thirds of the large hospital and the whole of the infectious hospital and there I believe they mean to stay for the next six months and they are so dirty the place is not the same.

We have very much indeed to feel thankful for and I hope after a time when we have been able to have a little rest and quiet that I shall feel better; at present I am very home sick and do so long for the children.

All food has gone up in price and I am just thinking of reducing our staff of servants and yet somehow it seems mean to turn them off when food will be a serious item for them.

All my visitors have gone home except Miss Herbert and Mr. Bradley and all the missionaries are commencing work again. The schools are very small for the capital is quite empty; the people are afraid to return to town. The P.M. is shut up in his grandson's house with a guard of soldiers round him and there he is to stay, the French say, until the people come back. We think that is only an excuse for keeping hold of him and probably he will be sent out of the island after a time.

The General is very strict and keeps the troops in very good order; there has been no looting. They are collecting all fire arms and even spears and putting them on a small island close to the French Residency, where they will be easily guarded. Look out for an account of the bombardment of Antananarivo in the Standard. Mr. Clark has sent an account of it and I expect it will interest you.

Willie is very busy but I hope he will be able to write to some of you. There are several wounded Malagasy in hospital and things require a great deal of looking after.

With much love to all our dear ones,
I am ever your loving sister
H. H. Wilson

In the country it was another story; many people had fled to the villages bewildered, unhappy and fearful of the future. The French had not yet established themselves in the out-lying districts and roving bands of Malagasy burnt and looted indiscriminately, turning to their old idols and bent on driving out any foreign elements. Christian missionaries who had been loved and respected were now suspect but some still had faith in the people round them and refused to abandon their stations. It was at this moment that William set off to visit Mandridrano where Mr. and Mrs. Standing were now living. They had three small children, and Mrs. Standing was ill and needed help. On the way he planned to call at the Friends Mission at Arivonimamo where William and Lucy Johnson were stationed. Hannah had written in the summer of a happy visit to their home telling Emmie about their small daughter, Blossom, who had a donkey to ride. She and Lucy Johnson had talked and sewn together during one holiday when Mary was a baby and when both mothers were recovering from fever. Bound by their many interests and difficulties they had formed a deep and lasting friendship.

These were anxious times, but William was unprepared for

*William Wilson on Merrylegs*

the tragedy which confronted him that day, as from a distant hill he looked down on the mission compound at Arivonimamo. Hannah writing to the children at home describes what happened :—

Father was on his way to Mandridrano; he started very early from here intending to have breakfast with the Johnsons, but when he got to the top of the hill about five miles from their home he saw a great crowd round the house and the school house and cottage hospital were in flames. He pushed on as hard as Merrylegs [his pony] could go to see if he could help Mr. Johnson, but when he got nearer to the house some one he knew met him and told him that Mr. Johnson was dead and that he must turn back at once;

but Father determined to go on. However after a time he was obliged to turn for people saw him and began running after him. They chased him for five miles or more and then gave it up. That night he started out with some friendly young men to go back to Arivonimamo, on foot and disguised as a native. After walking about nine miles and getting very nearly to the house they had to turn back again as it was not possible to get there without being discovered, two or three times they were nearly discovered as it was.

From three spies who had been sent out Father learnt that Mr. and Mrs. Johnson and little Lucy (Blossom) were all dead and had been buried by some of the servants. Father walked back the nine miles to the village where he had left his horse, intending to spend the night there – it was 12.30 a.m. when he got back and about 2.00 a.m. two of the young men came back from the village where they lived to tell him when they got home they found that people were to guard the roads at daybreak and to kill Father. He started off at once and these friends led him by bye-paths so as to avoid all villages and houses and by daybreak he was out of reach of the rebels. We must be very thankful darlings that God has spared dear Father to us, but oh! we do feel so sad! we don't know what we shall do without Mr. and Mrs. Johnson. Father is very tired and he has so many people coming to see him that he scarcely knows what to do. The Malagasy here in the town have been very kind to him, and such numbers have come and brought presents.

William, in a letter to his mother tells her that 'Hannah kept up bravely during the time of suspense and anxiety when I was away. Poor Hannah, she hardly thought to see me again alive!!'

After the tragedy at Arivonimamo, Malagasy Christians who were anxious for the safety of other missionaries sent an urgent message to Mandridrano telling the Standings of their danger. Fortunately Mrs. Standing was a little better, and with the help of sympathetic local people, the family and Ernest Robson, who was with them, were able to hide. No news could be sent to the waiting group in the capital until Dr. Ramorasata, who had taken William's place at the hospital, reported that he had been able to hold the local people together and prevent destruction for them and for the mission house. The Standings returned, but it was not considered safe for them to stay in such an isolated part of the country, and after some delay soldiers were sent to escort them to the capital; other missionaries too had narrow escapes and they would have been lost without the loyalty of their Malagasy friends.

During the next year order was slowly restored, with the Queen, still nominally head of the state but dominated by the French Resident, General Laroche, continuing to encourage her people and doing all she could to prevent bloodshed. At Christmas she visited the English Hospital where Hannah was resourcefully collecting presents for the forty-seven nurses and again arranging parties for them and for the students. Soon after Christmas William and Hannah moved to a house outside the compound but still at the foot of the hill and so near enough for William's work. It had a large garden with a mango grove at one end.

Anxious to be polite to the new French rulers the missionary wives paid calls on Mme. Laroche, the General's wife, and were much offended when she only returned the calls of the members of the Society for the Propagation of the Gospel. Hannah decided that she would never go again, and when she and William received an invitation to dinner, given in honour of the Queen and General and Mme. Laroche, they declined on the flimsy excuse that they did not like being out late at night. There was a growing feeling that these 'foreigners' did not like the English and the arrival of numbers of Jesuit priests made them afraid that Protestant missions were also unwanted. Several flourishing schools were closed and it was rumoured that some missionaries might be sent home.

In November 1896 the French took over the whole of the English Hospital, and William, now without this responsibility, established what almost amounted to a private practice in Antananarivo – now called Tananarive – as well as visiting and over-seeing medical work at the country missions. He was encouraged by the French many of whom were among his patients. His great regret was that students were no longer being trained at the hospital to help with the work in the country districts. There was still considerable unrest and when further rebellion broke out General Laroche was recalled, his last act being the official abolition of slavery in the island. General Galliéni, sent out in his place, put down rebellion with a firm hand, demanding the abdication of the Queen and declaring Madagascar a French colony.

Hannah grieved over the people whose villages were burnt; many had been caught up in a rebellion in which they had taken no part. Very little news came through in her letters at this time as she felt sure that they were opened, and there is no account from her of the deposing of the Queen, whom they all loved and who had so often entertained missionary wives and their children at the Palace.

Clara Herbert, who had travelled out with William and Hannah in 1882, had, over the years, become the Queen's most trusted friend, advising her and encouraging her in all her difficulties. It was from this friend that Hannah heard the story of those last days. When the Queen abdicated her one request was that she might take her crown with her into exile. This wish was granted, but when the crown was brought to her it was found to be a replica especially made of thin gold, so that it could be worn on long state occasions without tiring the wearer. Turning on the official who brought it, the Queen flung it on the floor and trampled on it, refusing all explanations. It was Clara Herbert who stooped to pick up two of the pitiful broken pieces which she later gave to Hannah and which confirmed her story. She kept in touch with the Queen and her aunt Princess Ramasindrazaney who was exiled with her, and visited them until, in 1917, the Queen died in Algeria, still a prisoner of the French Government.

*Two broken pieces of Queen Ranavalona's crown*

General Galliéni brought stability to the country round the capital and schools started again. Hannah gave English lessons and took sewing and knitting classes, also preparing work for the teachers in the country districts. On their journey out in 1894 they had called at Madeira and it must have been there that she bought the quantities of material and patterns which were used in the classes and proved so popular. During their first term of service she had introduced lace making, with local silk; it too was easily sold and of good quality but the industry gradually declined after the early workers gave it up. The Malagasy people have a tradition of craftsmanship and Hannah must have found her classes very rewarding. She introduced western crafts partly for their immediate use, but also because their sale at home would contribute to the mission funds. She and William appreciated the work which was native to Madagascar, and built up a collection of weaving which was both skilful and beautiful.

Though the country was quieter, food supplies were short and one letter speaks of chickens, once to be had at sixpence each and now 1/3d. The 'foreigners' – Hannah still identified herself fiercely with the people of the country – were responsible for making a famine of flour. She triumphantly laid in eighty pounds at nine pence a pound. Sugar was much the same price – it was shocking! One encouraging event was the arrival of two French protestants. They were very choice people, Hannah reports, and the possibility of another friendly mission was welcomed. The Jesuits on the other hand were angry at the intrusion into what they hoped would be an open field for their work, and continued to make trouble.

The event of 1897 was a visit to Mandridrano. William had been several times to see their old home and both he and Hannah longed to be in the country again. Bearers and palanquins were now difficult to find, but they preferred to ride, and William had purchased a mule for Hannah. On their way they stopped for some nights at Arivonimamo. Hannah had never seen the ruins of the happy home there, and she was so upset that she could not bring herself to tell of the visit in her letters. In spite of this sadness they could only respond wholeheartedly to the welcome they received, and for the children of the four nearest villages they organised a highly successful sports day. Prizes came out of the invaluable boxes sent by the Missionary Helpers Union at home, and every child was made happy by the gift of a bright new centime.

There was an even warmer welcome waiting for them in Mandridrano. Four hundred Sunday-school children gathered to greet them; former insurgents came to shake them by the hand, and there were the generous Malagasy gifts of poultry, rice and eggs and even a small pig. Hannah wrote to tell Lucy that her pet cat still came to the house for food, but had become adept at stealing; one day it ate half a pot of ointment without any apparent ill effect. William was soon busy with his medical work and for a whole month they welcomed visitors and made expeditions to outlying villages. Clara Herbert joined them to help with the requests for sewing and dressmaking lessons. The favourite country picnics were possible again, and one day they visited beautiful Lake Itasy, watching the crocodiles and finding a nest with over forty eggs hidden in the warm sand. Clara Herbert spent the best part of the day with Hannah, blowing these eggs as presents for the family at home. One, at least, is still treasured in its original wooden box padded with bright pink cotton wool. How one wishes one could have overheard the talk of the two ladies, as they worked at the eggs that day, laughing together over tales of crocodiles and past picnics. While they were there General Galliéni, 'our good Governor,' as William called him, came to see the schools. He appreciated the work which the missionaries had done in the outlying districts and was anxious that they should again try to penetrate the wilder parts of the country.

Once back in the capital work went on as before, William seeing up to 80 patients a day, and later, when plague threatened, he took an important part in the preparations against it. During a smallpox epidemic he personally vaccinated two thousand children. Hannah had now taken over the running of a small school; it is good to think that her training at Wigton and The Mount was useful and that her Malagasy, which she found so difficult had improved enough to make this possible. About this time she was also helping to visit and examine scholars in other nearby schools. The garden continued to flourish; they could never grow enough flowers, and roses and Cape lilies were welcomed when the cool weather returned. In this large garden there was plenty of room for the dogs and cats, and, among other pets, she reared a fascinating family of peacocks. Social life with many visitors continued and Hannah now had her 'at home' day. On the first afternoon she entertained nine guests including a French captain who arrived at seven o'clock in the evening, bringing photographs of his family to be admired. William came and went, making long journeys into the country. One Christmas day he got up at 6.30 and rode for three hours so that he might take a service. He rejoiced in the prospect of good roads which, alas, never fulfilled their promise, and he began to take a special interest in a new centre at Amboniriana, about forty miles from Tananarive.

Hannah remained in the capital, making their home a place of rest and refreshment for all who came. Then, in January 1899, the joy that she had so longed for came to her and another son, Robert Kenneth, was born. Her letters overflow with her delight in him, and with descriptions of his baby ways. He was a healthy child, though fear of the dreaded fever was never far away. Their Malagasy friends shared their pleasure and the baby was showered with gifts; a sheep, two turkeys, five geese, thirty or forty fowls and quantities of rice and eggs; generous indeed and a real help in a time of rising prices.

Happy and busy as she now was, Hannah still wished, with William, to be back in the country. The Mission station at Amboniriana was taking shape and a house was being built; there was already a garden under William's care. The planned move would be the fourth since their return to Madagascar, but with Kenneth growing and thriving they felt no call to remain in the city, and in November they were settled in the new home, happier than they had been since the days in Mandridrano. It would not be a long time of service, for they were to go on furlough at the end of the following year, but in the meantime they were among people for whom they cared so deeply. There were already some twenty-four congregations in their district.

For five years Hannah and their children in England had been 'famished on letters' as William's understanding

*Hannah Wilson with Kenneth, 1899*

biographer has written. In them Hannah had poured out her love, entering into all the children's joys and anxieties, worrying over recurring ailments, eager for news of their holidays, praising tidy writing and the little presents made with such care. The long intervals when mails were lost or held up could only be endured, as the need for their reassurance grew. One of their most faithful correspondents was William Cadbury, the second son of Richard. Besides writing, he sent them books and periodicals, and seeds for the garden. He felt especially sorry for the two little girls, Emmie and Lucy, left at home, visiting them and writing to them, and looking forward to the holidays which brought them to Birmingham to see their brother Alec. It was he who wrote to Hannah and told her of their doings, filling a gap as no one else seemed to do. Meanwhile his feeling for Emmie was becoming deeper as the years passed, and, in the year before their return, he wrote to William and Hannah telling them of the hope that one day she might be his wife, though he promised to wait until they came home and to talk with them then. In the meantime warm references to him in their letters to Emmie continued and it is impossible to feel that they were unsympathetic. Hannah was naturally anxious, as the aunts were becoming increasingly critical of this eldest daughter, but as she sat writing those last letters from Amboniriana she was full of quiet happiness.

William, wearing himself out to the last, was an anxiety, but she was heart and soul behind his work. He was already rebuilding the house at Arivonimamo, where they hoped to live when their furlough was over. He had some recreation in the country, for every journey brought the possibility of new birds or flowers, and he enjoyed duck shooting, bringing back supplies for the larder and adding to his collection of skins, shooting, before the days of modern photography, being the naturalist's accepted way of proving his discoveries. Even Hannah's sewing class of little girls, so clumsy after the more advanced pupils in Tananarive, was improving. It might pour with rain, but the new dahlias were in bloom and the garden was bright with many flowers. Baby Ken was disporting himself in a red frock to match the dahlias, and Emmie's much loved nurse, Neney, now with white hairs among the black, was there to hover round and see that he came to no harm. Above all there was the joyful certainty that the whole family would soon be together again. No wonder she was content.

In July of 1900 William and Hannah packed once more, and after a brief stay in Tananarive, said goodbye to their friends and started on the journey home.

Charles Senior had moved from Blackford to Weston-super-Mare hoping that the milder climate would benefit his ailing wife. There they had continued to make a home for Lucy and for Emmie now at The Mount School in York, who joined them for holidays, so it was natural that William and Hannah should take lodgings in Weston for a time, where the family could all stay together, and during the winter little Kenneth could become accustomed to the English climate. His Malagasy nurse was put into the starched cap and apron of an English nannie and was photographed with Kenneth on her knee so that she might show her people at home this strange costume. Their rooms were opposite a large church. One night they were all woken by the sound of muffled bells, tolling to tell them of the death of Queen Victoria.

Missionaries on furlough were in great demand both for speaking up and down the country and for committees in London, so for the next year the whole family lived in Winchmore Hill (now in north London). After six months William was asked to join a deputation to the Friends Syrian Mission Station in Brummana. Hannah was able to leave her family to join him for the return journey, when they visited Palestine and Egypt together. Watson Grace, the secretary of the F.F.M.A. had been one of the deputation, a comparatively young man who had already given ten years of outstanding service to the Association; on the way home he was taken ill and died shortly after reaching England. His death was a grievous loss and the Board asked William if he would take his place. William and Hannah had been expecting to return to the mission field, for in spite of the difficulties and sorrows of their service their hearts were still in Madagascar. They did not want to live and work in London, but the need there was urgent, and William agreed to take responsibility for two years before making a final decision. He was to remain at the central office at Devonshire House, Bishopsgate for the rest of his life.

*Queen Ranavalona in exile in Algeria*

Meanwhile William Cadbury's hopes had been happily fulfilled and it was in the Women's Meeting House of Devonshire House that he and Emmie were married on September 11th 1902.

Once the decision to remain in England was taken, William and Hannah settled in Hitchin, then a pleasant country town where a group of concerned Friends centred round a thriving Meeting. There Hannah took up the familiar pattern of William's work and travel, only now his journeys for the F.F.M.A. took him further afield. He made a long visit to workers in China and later, with Hannah, spent four happy months in Madagascar. In 1909 he was asked to go to India and Ceylon. His return journey would bring him to Marseilles, where William Cadbury planned to meet him with Hannah, Emmeline and Lucy. Before William's boat was due they crossed to Algeria where the deposed Queen of Madagascar was still living with Princess Ramasindrazaney. She was virtually a prisoner, but Hannah was given permission to visit her. There was a strict rule that she must never be left alone with her visitors, but the sympathetic French woman who kept watch over her explained this regulation and then added, 'But to-day I will take your daughters into the garden for a little while.' So the Queen and her aunt were left to talk in Malagasy with Hannah, while Emmeline and Lucy walked in the garden and picked tangerines with their kind hostess. Though no record of their conversation has remained, it surely brought some comfort to the exiled Queen as well as to Hannah, who cared so much for her and for her country.

Ranavalona III died in 1917. Clara Herbert was in touch with her to the last, and later wrote to Hannah, sending her a heavy gold brooch which held photographs of the Queen and her first greatly beloved husband. She had been mourning his early death when she succeeded to the Throne in 1883, and custom decreed that she must marry her detested Prime Minister.

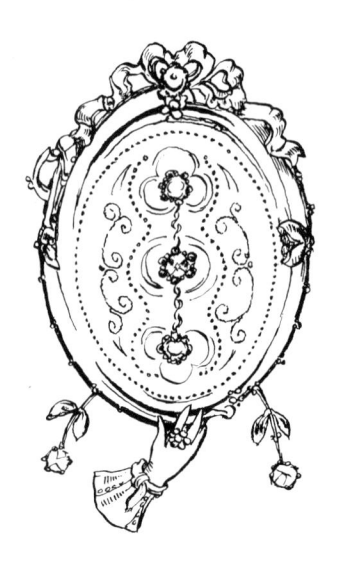

*Queen Ranavalona's brooch*

Clara Herbert wrote:–

This is the brooch that the late Queen Ranavalona prized more than any other. She and the Princess wore it continually. No one else ever has done so. Thou wilt know better than anyone what a treasure it was to them and I send it to thee with much dear love. Thou knowest that they sold most of their jewellery some years ago – for years they kept the brooch in the box sent.

Hannah, when passing it on to her daughter Emmeline, added that it was made of Malagasy gold by Malagasy craftsmen. Its design is French.

There was a happy re-union at Marseilles; though William had been seriously ill during his stay in Ceylon, the voyage had given him time to rest, and he seemed as well and full of life as ever. Hannah had always joined with him in his enthusiasm for the work he loved, and accepted his disregard for his own health. Her part was to be ready to welcome him, and to give him the rest and comfort that he needed when he came home. His sudden death in Hitchin that summer took him on a journey from which there could be no return and she was to be alone for the next thirty-six years; not immediately alone though, for Lucy, Alec and Ken were still with her at that time, while William Cadbury and Emmeline, now with three children of their own, were always ready to welcome her for visits and for family holidays, but nevertheless she remained lonely. Part of her heart was left in Madagascar, and, during these restless years, she journeyed to London for the monthly gatherings of Friends, and was a faithful member of the Madagascar and other committees.

The house in Hitchin, with William's last and most beautiful garden, held her for a time and then she moved to a Cadbury family house in Evesham, where she made happy holidays for many grandchildren. The garden there was full of fruit trees, and she would take a privileged child to the gardeners' store to find some special apple or pear. Children loved to be with her, accepting her sometimes exacting standards of manners. Her hair was soft and white, and she was an upright energetic figure in the black dresses which she always wore, but which never seemed out of place.

The years of the first World War brought changes to the family and anxieties to Hannah. Alec, who had emigrated to Canada some years earlier, returned to fight with the First Canadian Contingent. Mary who was teaching at the Quaker School at Mountmellick in Ireland, became engaged to the Rev. William Carroll and was married at Evesham in September 1916, returning to Ireland to live at Athy, in Co. Kildare.

In the meantime Alec had reached France, but after developing severe enteric fever was invalided home. He had planned to be at Mary's wedding to give her away, but was taken ill, and rushed into Birmingham on the wedding day for an operation for appendicitis; not content with this he developed measles. He was eventually discharged from the Canadian Army, and returned to France with a commission in the Royal Artillery; in spite of being gassed, he came back safely at the end of the war. Kenneth joined up in 1918 on his eighteenth birthday; was wounded after a short time at the front and did not go out to France again. Mary's husband served as a chaplain in Italy on a troop ship until 1921.

In 1922 Mary and Will Carroll with their small son Desmond, and Alec with his wife Denise, emigrated to Canada. Hannah was determined to visit them one day and finally set off with an old friend, Mrs. Roberts of Winchmore Hill, who was stone deaf. Together they had undertaken other journeys, Hannah being the active partner and managing the tickets and money which she always carried in an old fashioned linen pocket tied round her waist under her skirt. Grandchildren who travelled with her by train were fascinated to watch the way in which she turned her back to the passengers on a platform and deftly extracted the necessary notes; then, shaking her skirts into position, she would turn round again looking as if nothing had happened.

In 1928 she went to live in Birmingham so that she might be nearer to Emmeline. From here it was easy to reach her monthly committees. She still took a keen interest in all Madagascar affairs and particularly in young missionaries when they offered for service. She was now near their training college, Kingsmead, and could get to know them personally,

*William and Hannah Wilson with Kenneth
on their Silver Wedding day 1907*

later writing them the long letters that she knew would be welcome. Wherever she lived she attended and supported the nearest Friends' Meeting. A further move came when she went to Gerrards Cross to be near her sister Lizzie and within reach of day trains to London. It seemed that she could never settle for long in one place, and when her sister died in 1938, she went back to *Glenholme,* her father's house in Allendale. Her three unmarried sisters lived next door, and there were still many relations in the neighbourhood. *The Hope* had been let, but the rough shooting had been kept so that sons and grandsons who visited her could enjoy it. It was an ideal centre for holidays. The family came and found the same loving welcome and her gift of making a home wherever she might be.

During the second World War she stayed there; though hampered by her increasing deafness she could keep an eye on the sisters next door, welcome her visitors and write the letters which linked her with old friends. She could still do her beautiful knitting for the babies of the family and, in the evening, settle down to a game of patience, watched over and cared for by Mary Pitt, an old servant who had followed her to Northumberland, and who in those last years became a companion and friend. There in August of 1945 she died, and in the graveyard of Allendale Meeting they buried her, thanking God for her life of love and service; a life that had begun among the bracing hills of Northumberland. Now, after all her journeys, she had come home.

*Hannah Wilson, c.1935*

CHAPTER III

# EMMELINE HANNAH CADBURY
# 1883 – 1966

## The Third Hannah

Daughter of Hannah Henderson and William Wilson
Married William Adlington Cadbury 1902

ONE FEBRUARY DAY IN 1887 there was great excitement in the missionary house in Antananarivo, the capital of Madagascar, which was Emmie's first home. A large parcel had arrived from England, and the family were unpacking it together. Three year old Emmie, her eyes bright and her curls clinging damp on her forehead was diving into the box, while her father knelt on the floor beside her, and her mother sat near with baby Ashlin on her knee.

What loving thoughts had gone into the packing! There were books and medicines for William, Emmeline's father; calico, cottons, needles and buttons for her mother, and for Emmie herself new summer socks and gloves; gloves made of fine white cotton, the first she had ever seen. She was dancing out of the door to show them to Neney, her Malagasy nurse, when a packet appeared marked with her name. As she opened it, it made an unexpected little noise, and the next moment she held a doll in her arms; a doll with eyes that opened and shut and which cried like a real baby. Nothing would stop her now; she was off to the kitchen where the whole household gathered to see her wonderful present. The Malagasy servants were as charmed and mystified as she was by the strange human sounding voice, and Emmie, the centre of all attention, proudly showed off the shining yellow curls and blue eyes, and turned her treasure over and over that everyone might hear it cry again. Her father, fondly looking on, laughed as he watched the little fluttering fingers in the new gloves, and when he next wrote to his mother, said that 'they as well as her stockings have not failed to give her full gratification, for if there is anything the little rogue likes it is a little bit of finery or new things'.

Emmie had been a tiny baby and she remained small for her age but she developed fast. Her hair grew soft and fluffy, her eyes deepened to hazel and could sparkle with delight or darken with displeasure when anything went wrong. Once on her feet she trotted about, busy as a little girl can be. Her small precise fingers experimented with all that came her way; mud, sticks, leaves and fallen blossoms, as well as the toys which found their way into the warmth of the tropical garden. Her mind opened too, and she began to talk in a quaint mixture of two languages, Malagasy being the first in which she was fluent, or 'glib', to quote her father.

She was two years old when her brother Ashlin was born: old enough to realise her mother's grief when he died so suddenly of the dreaded fever. She learnt then to help and comfort Hannah in her own way, and an enduring bond grew up between them. When another baby was expected Emmie joined in all the preparations, and would watch eagerly for the arrival of the parcels which brought Hannah the materials she needed – white cottons for summer because in those days colours faded so quickly in the hot sun. For winter, when winds could be chilly, she asked for thin woollen stuffs in dark colours. In January of 1886 there had been a special party and Hannah had been greatly exercised over Emmie's dress for such an important occasion. Fortunately a length of blue nunsveiling, a thin woollen material, had lately come from England, and there was enough to make a dress with two frills; feather stitching in white silk completed the trimming and there were white socks and black shoes to wear with it. For her head there was nothing better than a calico bonnet which Hannah edged with everlasting lace. She would never have risked making Emmie vain, but she wrote an account of her contrivings for a sister, and in the privacy of a letter admitted that the child 'looked very bonny'. How Emmie must have enjoyed all the fuss and planning and the more than satisfactory results. Her father himself took pleasure in seeing his little daughter so beautifully dressed and was delighted when a friend admired the pretty frock, remarking that most missionary off-spring looked like old maid's children, but Hannah was not entirely satisfied and no time was lost in writing for a shady hat for special occasions. The requests for necessities continued. Shoes were a problem, as those made in Madagascar lost their shape so quickly, but eight pairs for the

*Emmie with her shady hat – Antananarivo, 1890*

two children could be sent from England and cost £1. In one letter £6 was enclosed for a variety of requests, but William looking over the list crossed off nainsook, a fine cotton material, which Hannah wanted so badly for Sunday pinafores, and for handkerchiefs to fit little pockets.

When at last Lucy Mary arrived no one was more delighted than Emmie.

## Mandridrano

Nothing can match Emmie's own account of her childhood or of the journey they then took to her second home in Mandridrano; though notes, written many years later with artless fidelity for her father's biographer, were printed, to her dismay, just as she had recorded them.

Life for Emmie was filled with new pleasures and all her happiest memories of Madagascar centred round this country home. She loved the space and freedom of the bare compound which surrounded the house, with stables and cowshed a little distance away. Here she could be safely left under watchful Malagasy eyes, with all the wonderful natural playthings that belong to country children. Best of all her father's work at this time was based on his home and when he could be spared from the calls of church and people he was an absorbing companion, always full of plans for the garden, experimenting, planting and observing; no wonder she loved to be with him. She pottered round him as he worked, and together they would plan surprises for her mother, and come in from the garden, Emmie bursting with some new secret.

Growing up in this far away country her life was rich with experiences that at the time seemed everyday happenings, but which wove a background of colour for the rest of her life. Scarlet poinsiettas, arum lilies, plumbago with its delicate blue flowers, and heavy scented tuber roses remained as dear to Emmie as the violets and primroses of home, and to her all flowers were as precious as those first ones that she learnt to love with her father. From him, too, she inherited a daring urge to experiment. Later, with her own children she delighted to share the escapades which never appeared in her written account of those days. For instance the anxious Malagasy servants warned her that if she sucked the tough outer skin of a pineapple her tongue would swell up and she would die, whereupon she immediately set to work to prove them wrong. More dangerous was the fascination of the forbidden chillies with their tempting scarlet fruits, for after picking them she rubbed her eyes, and was nearly blinded by their stinging juices.

There is no record of the numbers of helpers employed at Mandridrano, but Helen Gilpin, the headmistress of the big girls school in Antananarivo, is recorded in 1892 as having a household of six to do the work: including a housewoman, serving woman, cook, houseman, a third man to do rough housework and a children's caretaker, who presumably minded the combined families of the other servants. The Wilsons of course would have had nurses for the children as well, besides men to care for the horses and cows.

William was a born naturalist, and was fascinated by the wild life around him. He kept many pets, among them lemurs, strange creatures of the forest, unique to Madagascar. The two which had been brought to him had soft grey fur and tails ringed with black and white; one became quiet and friendly, but one remained fierce and unreliable, and Emmie, looking for mischief, dared little Mary to run within reach of its chain; Mary obediently ran and was badly bitten. Another favourite pet was a baby crocodile, but this was considered so unlucky that it was killed by the faithful cook. When her father shot a twenty-foot crocodile it was another matter, and everyone gathered round in hope of getting some of the desired fat. Emmie insisted on sitting astride the tail as it was skinned, until she was saturated with its strong musky smell, and her mother carried her off to the veranda to be washed from head to foot.

This crocodile had been shot on one of the many expeditions to Lake Itasy. There were so many to be found there in those days that two canoes had to be lashed together before it was considered safe to venture on the water. There was great jubilation when nests of eggs were found on the sandy shore. These picnics were the one time when mother and children left the mission station, and to celebrate a holiday the whole establishment would pack up and set off in the early morning for some favourite spot. Everyone enjoyed these expeditions and there was much laughing and running to and fro as the supplies for the day were packed into baskets and panniers, and the Malagasy carrying-chairs were brought out for Hannah and the children, while William rode beside them.

There was another side to this happy life to which Emmie's father and mother were so deeply committed, a side which influenced the children in ways which no one could estimate, and the anxieties of her parents were absorbed unconsciously by the little girl; she realised her mother's loneliness when her father rode off on his long and dangerous journeys into the wild unexplored country to the south of Mandridrano, where the fierce independent men of the Sacalava tribe, who grazed their cattle there, resented these missionary intrusions which were being encouraged by the Christian Queen of Madagascar; Emmie anxiously watched her mother's face when messengers arrived with news of her father's progress, but sometimes there was no news for weeks together.

As we know, William although at this time not a qualified doctor, was steadily building up a reputation as a healer and with growing experience was establishing what was later to become a small hospital. In spite of his sympathetic care, his successes roused the antagonism of some of the local people. They said nothing openly, but the mission servants were uneasy, and William with his fluent Malagasy realised that there were many prejudices and fears to be overcome. One dreadful day he returned from a long journey so ill with fever that he had to be helped from his horse and almost carried upstairs to bed. This was the moment that had been waited for with such patience, and when night fell there were eerie tappings at the windows, as the witch doctors, made bold by the 'stranger's' illness, crept up to the house and tried to charm away his life. An indignant Neney held Emmie close, assuring her that the house was well guarded; the faithful cook only made matters worse by firing blank cartridges and waking Mary in her cot, and as long as William lay ill the evil remained tangible. To the end of her life Emmie feared the dark, and moonlight held no charms for her; perhaps the moon had been shining during that first night of her father's fever.

Because of the isolation and uncertainty both parents were all the more determined to make a loving stable centre in their home. Sunday evenings were always spent together, and if William was away on a journey, Hannah and the little girls would think of him as they sang the hymns that they had learnt with him. Then certain small treasures, among them delicate Swiss figures carved with unbelievable skill, were brought out, telling of another far-away world. How Emmie longed for the perilous delight of holding them in her own small hands. At these times, the family in England was remembered and stories were told of Hannah's home, high up in the hills of Northumberland and they repeated the names of the relations from whom letters and parcels came so faithfully. Sure in the love of those distant grandmothers, uncles and aunts the little family in Madagascar could never be entirely cut off or forgotten. There was support too, from the devoted men and women who encouraged her parents in their service, and to Emmie the 'Board', the govening body of the Friends Foreign Missionary Association, about which they talked so often, stood for something strong and dependable; ready to help them in Madagascar, and to welcome them when the time came for them to return to England.

They had now lived in Mandridrano for two years and the promised furlough was not so very far away. Emmie was nearly six years old. She could sew and knit and crochet a little, but it seems that she had been given no regular lessons, and much preferred to follow her father about, or to ride her mother's pony. In May they moved back to the capital to recover from fever, always particularly bad in Mandridrano, and to gain strength for the journey home. There was a warm welcome from the missionary community waiting for all the family, with parties for Emmie and Mary as well as for their parents, but Emmie sadly missed the freedom of a country station, and even more the happy hours spent with her father: she must now go to school and it is easy to imagine that children's books of those days had little in common with the life she knew. She was always a friendly little girl and gladly joined the little group in the city, but she missed her old playmates, the country animals, and when in July she was six years old she begged for a little pig to keep as a pet. Her mother, fearing that she had run wild too long, and wanting her to care for pretty feminine things, made her a handkerchief case of red satin, and trimmed it with an edging of lace; however, when Emmie woke on her birthday morning the first thing that she heard was a snuffling sound which came from a basket under her bed.

That September they left for England, with a new brother Alec, who had arrived in August. The journey passed safely, and when they reached London members of the Board were at the station to meet them. Little Emmie looked up into a bearded face and holding fast to a large comfortable hand, felt that they did indeed promise the security that she would need in the strange noisy world that was so bewildering.

## England

The first months in England passed in a rush of new sights and sounds. Hannah was a farmer's daughter, and her home in Allendale brought dear familiar delights for her, while the names so long talked about and known from letters became kind faces for the children. A journey to Birmingham for Christmas took them to an enormous house, where they received a loving welcome from Emmie's Aunt Emma, her father's sister married to Richard Cadbury, and their large family. Two sons, Barrow and William, were still at home with five daughters, Jessie, Edith, Helen, Daisie and Beatrice.

The little girl felt overwhelmed by the crowd of new relations, and took refuge with a shy young man who was, she learnt, her cousin William. On Christmas day there was a family party with much present giving. One visiting aunt, Aunt Elsie, after unwrapping an especially precious piece of china all packed in shavings, suddenly noticed that she had lost another present, a ring which had been given to her that morning. What a hubbub there was as everyone offered suggestions, with the children turning over the paper and ribbons that littered the floor. Emmie, watching from her new cousin William's knee,

*Emma Cadbury – William's sister, c.1876*

suddenly slipped down and timidly went up to the formidable visiting aunt. 'I think' she said 'that your ring might have come off in all those shavings'. The aunt knelt down beside her, 'What a good idea' she cried, 'Do you think you could try to find it for me?' Then Emmie who knew so much about boxes and parcels forgot all her shyness, joyfully plunged her arms into the shavings, and while a group of noisy cousins looked on, she found the ring! Aunt Elsie, George Cadbury's wife might look formidable, but she loved and understood children, and she had made a frightened little girl very happy; Emmie always remembered her kindness with gratitude. She began to feel at home, and was not at all abashed when that evening they all laughed at her when she refused the unusual treat of a banana. 'No thank you' she said decidedly, remembering Madagascar where fruit was never allowed at supper, 'I don't want to get fever'. After the excitement of Christmas it was a relief when the whole family settled down in London where William was to spend the next four years qualifying as a doctor. Emmie and Mary, who was now to be known by her first name of Lucy, began to get used to English ways and English weather, while Alec practised his first steps in the nursery.

All went well until the following year when letters began to fly between the aunts and Emmie's mother. They all knew that one day homes would have to be found for the three older children, as they would need to stay in England for the sake of their health and education when their parents returned to Madagascar, but no-one had thought other needs would arise so soon. Now, however, Emmie's mother was expecting another child and would not be able to manage three children and a new baby in the small London house, so something would have to be done to help her.

William Wilson's eldest sister Hannah, married to Charles Senior, a minister of the Church of England who held the living of Blackford near Carlisle, came to the rescue. Hannah already had a large family, three grown-up step-children, Arthur, Caroline and Hilda, and a son Charlie and a daughter Dorothy who was just Emmie's age. After much anxious thought, they suggested that Emmie should come at once to Blackford, and that when her parents left England she should make her home there. It was a generous offer, and was gladly accepted, for it seemed the best possible arrangement. The last year had seen many changes, and the break in the family was bound to come, so with promises of holidays together in Allendale, Emmie was given into the care of this kind aunt, who was to be a mother to her for the next eight years.

Eager to love and be loved Emmie adapted herself to the new life. Dorothy welcomed her gladly, and they soon became fast friends, learning their lessons together, repeating the collect for the day each Sunday, attending church, and helping to give out the parish magazine, a special treat which meant calling at all the houses in the village. The vicarage is still there, a comfortable red brick Victorian house with a cedar in the garden. The country is flat with few trees and must have been bleak in winter, but there was plenty going on in the busy family life which Emmie shared. The boys, Arthur and Charles, came and went, but Carrie, who had to spend three years on her back after a bad fall, remained at home together with Hilda, who, energetic and capable, gave lessons to the two little girls.

In the summer of 1892 came the joyful news of the arrival of another brother, Samuel Basil, and a month later the family all met in Allendale, staying at grandfather Matthew Henderson's farm *The Hope*. How good it was to be with her father and mother and the little ones again. Basil was a dear baby, and Alec sent them all into gales of laughter with his funny little ways; it was indeed a happy time, and Allendale became dearer at each visit. One of Emmie's pleasures was to sit beside her grandmother, Hannah Henderson, listening to the stories of her young days. Best of all was the tale of the great-grandmother, Mary Hall, who had run away one summer evening to be married at Gretna Green to great-grandfather Isaac Hall. Geordie Graham, the son of the farm man John, behind whom she had ridden on that eventful journey, was still working at *The Hope*. This made it all seem very real and near. A Wilson great-grandmother had also eloped with her husband, and Emmie wondered whether there would be any possibilities for her; she thrilled at the thought of galloping away through the night.

It may have been during this holiday that Emmie's parents began to talk to her about the new changes that were bound to come. They expected to leave England in October taking Basil with them, but plans for her and Lucy were to be altered, involving another move for Emmie and leaving Lucy behind at Blackford. She was shattered at this news. 'Where shall I go?' she cried despairingly, 'why must I leave Dorothy? Dorothy is my friend and she won't want to do lessons with little Lucy.' As cheerfully as they could her parents explained their new plan.

Two of their dearest friends in Madagascar, Henry Clark and his wife (Dadabe and Mummy to the children), had a brother, Joseph Firth Clark, who lived in Doncaster, and it was he and his wife who had invited Emmie to stay with them. He had two sons a little older than Emmie, Oswald and Bernard, and a daughter Nannie who, like Dorothy, was just her age. He sent kind messages, hoping so much that she would be happy with them; it must have been a hard struggle to accept this plan, but Emmie, like her mother, was always fiercely loyal to those she loved, and she tried bravely to be all that her father and mother would wish. She had two more months with Dorothy, and then they had to say goodbye. One sadly distressed little note, hastily written on the day she arrived in Doncaster, and smudged with tears, must have come near to breaking her mother's heart, but she responded to the loving new uncle and aunt, and to the joys of a family life with big brothers as well as a sister, and before Christmas was full of the delights of winter. Oswald and Bernard were building a snow house in the garden and they had all been given a half-holiday for a wonderful skating party. Emmie hardly knew how to express her happiness, and wrote that the cold weather was awfully jolly, with the trees all covered with frost. Everything seemed to be praising God, and everybody was so kind. 'I feel so thankful I can't help it [she wrote], "For his mercies shall endure, ever faithful ever sure", is true I think.' Her father's delight in life, and her mother's simple faith were helping her more than she knew.

Emmeline blossomed in this Quaker home, less conventional than the life of Blackford but still centred round a deep Christian loyalty. The whole family went to Meeting each Sunday, and visiting Friends would discuss their concerns over Sunday dinner. Mission work, adult education and the Temperance witness in Doncaster were absorbing topics. The children might listen in silence, but to Emmie the talk was familiar. She felt secure and happy, and it is good to think that she was with such understanding friends when the sad news came that little Basil had died of fever soon after his arrival in Madagascar. It all seemed so far away but Emmie's loving heart knew how to send messages of comfort to her mother.

Meanwhile in Blackford and Birmingham the aunts had not

forgotten their responsibilities. Next summer Aunt Emma invited Emmie and Lucy to stay with her at *Winds Point*, the Cadbury family's house on the Malvern Hills, and she included Dorothy Senior and Nanny Clark in the invitation. Some time was spent with Aunt Hannah Senior and there was always a welcome in Allendale, but Emmie's home was now in Doncaster with the Clarks and Joseph Firth could write to her father that she was like one of their own children, and that her presence was a blessing in the house. Did Aunt Hannah feel that Emmie was losing her dependence on her own relations? Whatever the cause she was determined to care for the child personally and after two years found strength to insist on her return to Blackford for Christmas, though the Clarks were reluctant to let her go. The outcome of this visit settled the question of Emmie's return to Blackford and she heard the news with consternation. 'I am so sorry to leave Doncaster' she wrote. 'Auntie I must come back for holidays, and for the whole holidays next Easter. You will write and say so won't you?' But Aunt Hannah was firm, and except for that one Easter Emmie never visited the Clarks again. She must understand that her home was at Blackford and that holiday invitations from relations came first.

Emmie slipped back into the familiar life at the Rectory with bright little Lucy to join in the weekly routine. Sundays were happy and less restricted than might have been expected. At dinner the children were encouraged to remember the text of their uncle's sermon, and if they were successful were given a penny, though it seemed a little hard that this had to be put into the missionary box. On Sunday afternoons the table was cleared, papers were spread and out came pens and paint boxes, Sunday letters were written and many little cards were ornamented with texts, pictures, or pressed flowers from the rectory garden and sent to the far-away mother and father. As Christmas came round small presents were stitched with loving care and were accompanied on their long journey by Aunt Hannah's comments on the children's progress. Another feature of Sunday, remembered by Lucy, was the unalterable menu for the Sunday dinner which greeted them on their return from Morning Service; cold beef with mashed potatoes, followed in winter by bread and butter pudding, while in summer a salad was added to the beef, and cornflour mould with stewed fruit took the place of a hot pudding. Many families of those days must have been restricted by the limited repertoire of their very plain cooks, and their distrust of expensive sauces and relishes which came in suspect bottles, or, even worse, in tins. Good wholesome food was made at home, and the annual marmalade making turned the Rectory upside down. Meals became even simpler, the children were given a holiday, and everyone was pressed into cutting orange peel into the same thin even slices, while the sharp tang of the fruit filled the air and great preserving pans full of the first boilings sizzled on the stove. Emmie remembered it all to the end of her life and liked to help with her daughters' marmalade-making, though she distrusted modern methods.

Emmie and Lucy were fortunate indeed in an aunt who loved them, and if they sometimes felt lost or misunderstood how could they know of her feelings of anxious responsibility, complicated by the conflicting advice of her sisters. Her personal problems, too, were far from simple. Standards for the family of a clergyman were high, and both sons must attend university and be started in a career. It was to Hilda's clear head that she turned for help and advice in house-keeping and other financial matters. Hannah had some money of her own, and when her brother William was at home, could consult him about her investments, but she was in real difficulty when dividends fell short one year owing to a strike in a mine in which she had shares. Also as the oldest of the Wilson family she felt it her duty to care for other relatives who were finding life difficult. Her mother was well provided for by Richard Cadbury, but an elderly aunt had no-one to support her, and Hannah roused herself to write to her sisters to beg them to promise a shilling or 1/6d a week to provide simple extras; she even wrote to William in Madagascar, and to the nieces at Uffculme for their help. She spent her brother William's allowance for his children with scrupulous care and took great pleasure in the pretty dresses she contrived for them. 'Lucy has been asked to sing in a school concert' she wrote on one occasion. 'She will wear the white silk frock that Beatrice had for Edith Butler's wedding, it fits her nicely and with fresh chiffon on the collar and Malagasy lace in the sleeves which come to the elbow, and long cream gloves and white shoes and stockings and a white ribbon in her hair she looks very nice and pretty.'

In the schoolroom Hilda now faced her problems, and Emmie one more change in her education. Lessons began with added urgency, for it was already planned that she should follow her mother to The Mount School in York in a years time, when she would be fourteen years old and Nannie Clark could join her there. She was a sad puzzle to her conscientious cousin who found her bright and intelligent in subjects which interested her, Natural History, English and Geography, but who complained that her mind became a perfect blank when faced with Arithmetic or Grammar. 'All she does has to be drummed into her head,' cried exasperated Hilda. 'She needs to know what *work* means, for what she learns one day she often quite forgets the next.' For Spelling and Music there seemd no hope at all. However, there was one bright spot: Hilda herself loved history and took comfort in reading Julius Caesar aloud on two evenings a week, 'because the children enjoyed it so much', and this abiding interest was effortlessly passed on to Emmie. Still the fear remained that although she would be happy in the companionship of school, she would learn nothing; was Emmie already taking refuge in 'being stupid', always her excuse for failure as she grew older? She does not seem to have taken her lessons very seriously, but there was one way in which she excelled; she could sew beautifully. When her cousin Charlie was going up to Oxford for his first term he needed six new shirts. Here was a splendid chance for Emmie to show her skill, while plain sewing would occupy her fingers and teach her the value of diligence. She was always a favourite with all her boy cousins, and liked to please them, so she willingly undertook the tedious task of sewing two long seams for each shirt, finishing them with gussets at each side. Alas! She was not at all satisfied when as a reward Aunt Hannah gave her 1/6. Even for Charlie's sake she felt that this was poor thanks for hours of uninteresting work. She had hoped to frame a cherished picture of Queen Victoria in something infinitely more worthy than the plain unvarnished wood which was all that she could now afford.

*Emmie, thirteen years old*

Life at Blackford was enlivened by holidays; other relations were anxious to do their part in caring for the Wilson children and each summer Emmie and Lucy continued to visit their Henderson grandparents in Allendale, where they met an increasing number of cousins. There were endless drives in the pony-trap to visit other farming relatives, and later long bicycle rides over the high fell roads which plunged down into valleys with clear-flowing streams. Under the wide windy skies of this border country Emmie learnt the names of the heathers that grew there, and she specially loved the bog plants and mosses and the ferns that were everywhere. There were expeditions to pick bilberries and blackberries, and much picnicking. Even in old age, remembering those days, and many family holidays of other years, she would stop the car and choose to eat her sandwiches in open places, indifferent to cold and damp.

At Christmas-time the little sisters joined Alec at Uffculme. There was a large nursery with room for any number of children and Dorothy was often included in the invitation. Aunt Hannah shook her head over the luxury that prevailed there, feeling that her sister lived to spend money on herself and her four daughters; what a bad example it was for Emmie and Lucy who would always have to be careful. For their part the children took everything for granted, and during those early Christmas visits joined happily in all the festivities, making no comparisons. Beatrice, a year younger than Emmie, was like a welcoming sister, and her much older brother William made special friends with all three little girls. He wrote to them when they returned to Blackford, always including Dorothy when sending them small presents. He talked to Emmie and Lucy and Alec about their father and mother in Madagascar, and began to send reports of their visits with accounts of their progress in his letters to these distant parents. He had become keenly interested in William Wilson's work in the mission field. Someone has said of him that he was a great romantic, and loyal as he was to his part in the family firm, he must at times have longed for a more adventurous life and envied William Wilson his opportunities in an almost unknown country. With the letters he sent books and papers as well as tools and seeds for the garden, and on hearing of an outbreak of plague he supplied money and drugs at a time when Friends in London were having to cut down their support.

The only brother remaining at home in a family of talkative sisters, he must sometimes have felt lonely, though he joined in the active life of the large group of young Friends in Birmingham. The cycling club held many rallies and parties, as did the Friends Reading Society, and he played cricket and golf, but for holidays he often went by himself to sail with local fishermen up and down the west coast of Ireland, developing a deep love and sympathy for the people there. 'That is where you find the real Kings of Ireland' he would say.

As the years passed his interest in his little cousins deepened, and for Emmie he began to have a special care. In telling about those early times she remembered a Boxing Day walk into the country when he picked a piece of holly and pinned it in her cap. They had taken a train to King's Norton, walking over the fields and down into Alvechurch; the spray of holly had come from a tree growing by a farm pond that they passed on the way. She was only nine years old, but it was during that holiday that he made up his mind that one day she should be his wife.

Something has been told of William Cadbury's love for Emmie and their eventual marriage but the details of his long years of patient waiting belong to her story.

When the time came for Emmie to go to The Mount in January 1898, William Cadbury, knowing of the family's financial difficulties offered to pay her fees. Aunt Hannah, who already had some inkling of his growing affection, wrote to Madagascar of his goodness and generosity, and of her feeling of shame that he should have to help when others could have taken the responsibility. She was thinking of her sister Emma, but she had already given Alec a home and probably felt, with some justification, that she had done her share. No other solution seemed possible, and William Cadbury's offer was accepted. Aunt Hannah somehow found the necessary school requirements, and from the first Emmie was happy at York; she made many friends, and true to Hilda Senior's prediction she enjoyed all the ups and downs of boarding school life in the two years she spent there. Lessons were another story, for she never completely left the bottom class and yet in spite of her 'stupidity' she learned widely; this was shown by her constant success in the general knowledge paper which everyone took at the end of each year; in her final term she came first.

Christmas visits to Birmingham continued, and in December of 1897 everything seemed to conspire to add to the excitement. Carrie Senior came with them on the long journey, to stay with their Wilson grandmother, William's mother', while Emmie, Lucy and Dorothy were all with Alec at Uffculme, the big house which Richard Cadbury had built so that he might be nearer to Bournville. Edith (Richard and

*Emmie aged fifteen*

Emma's eldest daughter), had been married that year, and her husband, Arnold Butler was a great favourite, while young Richard, at home for the holiday, was becoming fond of Carrie and rejoiced to have her nearby. Romance was in the air, and Emmie could tell of many times when she was invited by some member of the family to make a third for walks, a necessary propriety in those days. She was still so small that they thought of her as a child, but their little cousin was old enough to be useful. 'Emmie will make such a good wife for a poor man' remarked Arnold one day, when they were all having tea in the nursery. Emmie, who had been helping to carry plates and cups, felt that they would never realise that she was growing up. The yellow stockings, which were the only present given to her that Christmas by her Aunt Emma were another painful example; not only were they childish, but they were ugly. Emmie was quite old enough to long for pretty clothes and to envy the many new dresses of the Cadbury sisters. She turned to her cousin William knowing that she could count on his understanding and sympathy, and with him she felt no restraint. She loved to walk with her hand in his, and in passionate gratitude she flung her arms round his neck and kissed him to thank him for his present.

Unaware that her cousins had been watching and criticising her, Emmie began her first term in York at The Mount, and her letters home were full of her doings. A lecture by Nansen, the great explorer, thrilled her; she was developing her feeling for history and was deep in the story of *Two Noble Lives*,

*Emmie at The Mount, 1898*

while Natural History was another subject which caused no difficulties. The school believed in regular excursions into the country and that springtime she revelled in the primroses at Castle Howard. Later in the term she reported that two very good 'Friendish Friends' were holding meetings at the school, and that they had two long ones each day; at least there was variety in life at The Mount. She was always ready to absorb anything that came her way, but she never forgot her parents and grieved for her mother and the lost baby brother. 'Oh Auntie dear' she wrote to Aunt Hannah, 'I can't bear to think that she is so lonely and yet we cannot help it.' She cried over her father's letters, and a little gold brooch shaped like a geranium leaf was treasured because he had asked a Malagasy goldsmith to make it for her. Emmie's heart might ache, for she missed her parents deeply, but they had now been gone for four long years, and, by the end of her letter to her aunt, her natural lively reactions to life reasserted themselves, and she wrote that she was 'wild' with a Quakerly member of the staff who would not let her class lean out the window to watch the Black Watch Regiment go marching by with bagpipes playing and kilts swinging. She ended with an uninhibited request, 'Please will you send me some more MONEY. It goes'.

That happy Christmas at Uffculme was to have wide repercussions for them all. Barrow and Jessie, William's older brother and sister were married as well as Edith, but Helen and Daisy, next in age had watched all that went on between their brother William and Emmie and finally complained to their mother in shocked whispers. 'Just look mother' they said, 'How loverishly William and Emmie are behaving.' Emma dismissed their ideas as nonsense, but she began to watch for herself, and to feel anxious. After a long talk with William, her stepson, it became clear that her fears were justified, that his hopes and intentions were fixed, and that he was ready to write to Emmie's parents then and there. Emma was horrifed; his love for this childish unimportant little niece was the last thing that she and her daughters had imagined or wanted, so she persuaded him to wait until she herself broke the news to Emmie's parents.

It was not until August in the calm of a summer holiday in Cornwall that she found courage to write to Madagascar, and while assuring her brother of her love for Emmie, bewailed the sixteen years that separated her in age from William, feeling that what he needed and longed for was marriage now and a home of his own. As a very eligible bachelor in the large group of Friends in Birmingham, she had every reason to believe that he could be married most suitably if only he would forget this unfortunate infatuation.

Aunt Hannah, who had also received a letter quoting the unmentionable word 'loverish', felt hot and angry and wrote at once to Madagascar to defend Emmie, furious that she had not been gently told that she was too old for childish behaviour. What an example she had when all the girls kissed Arnold, Edith's husband. Why! Daisy had even been seen sitting on his knee. This loving aunt had watched William Cadbury herself and for sometime had realised his feelings; her great fear was that Emmie's innocent love and trust might be hurt by disagreements; this above all she prayed might be avoided.

The sisters at least agreed that William and Emmie must see less of each other, and it was fortunate that the summer holiday in Allendale had already been planned. The Senior family had lately moved to Weston-Super-Mare, in the hope that a milder climate would help Aunt Hannah's continuing ill health. Allendale was now a long way off, and, at the end of the holiday there, Emmie and Lucy arrived in Weston completely exhausted by the fourteen hour journey. To make matters worse they had not been put into a ladies' compartment and as there were no corridors in those days, had travelled, as they said, 'with a silly old man and his keeper', who had talked to them till he left the train at Gloucester. No wonder Aunt Hannah was upset and blamed the thoughtless relation who had put them on the train at Carlisle, without apparently seeing anything wrong in the arrangement.

Once safely back at Weston, Aunt Hannah's worries increased, for Emmie developed a slight swelling in her neck, and fearful, as were all her generation, of tubercular glands, she called in her doctor. He diagnosed 'a touch of Derbyshire neck', or thyroid trouble, which he thought would soon subside. He was more concerned by a slight dilation of the heart and possible anaemia and thought that the long bicycle rides, which she had enjoyed so much in Allendale, had caused some strain. He ordered iron and arsenic pills and extra food, and suggested that she should not return to The Mount for a few weeks. William Cadbury came for a short visit and, according to Aunt Hannah, kept himself 'wonderfully in hand, paying attention to Carrie as a sort of blind', but Emmie was not entirely taken in; Cousin William was still her dearest friend.

Meanwhile pleasant undemanding activities were planned to fill her day. In the morning she was given *The Life of Wellington* – a good sensible book – to read for half-an-hour, and then she practiced her music for an hour, without much energy or interest; after that she was allowed to read stories, and to amuse herself as she liked, resting when she felt tired. She was encouraged to be out of doors as much as possible, and found consolation in the family pug, Twopence, who needed exercise.

It was not intended to be a stimulating programme; fortunately Lucy and Dorothy were there to provide companionship and amusement, while Carrie was resourceful and sympathetic; Emmie could still take a keen pleasure in watching her limited world with observant eyes.

> Madge and Willie [Wilson cousins] came to tea [she wrote to her mother]. We had games in the garden first, then tea. After that we took Auntie on to the esplanade in her chair; the sea was simply beautiful, it was very calm, the sky was red with the setting sun, and the sea reflected the colour with tiny ripples of gray [sic], and great lines of gray tipt [sic] with red where the waves came bending in to brake in white foam on the shore and rocks, we stayed and watched it for sometime . . .

Emmie's spelling might be poor but her letters had already the gift of natural expression that they never lost.

Poor Aunt Hannah had other anxieties. Her stepson Arthur Senior, after a short blissful engagement lost all hope of marriage when his future wife was taken dangerously ill; then came the news of Carrie's engagement to young Richard Cadbury who was to take her to live in South Africa, and there was a wedding to plan. It is to be hoped that Emmie was able to help and to join in the preparations as, to add to her aunt's troubles, she was still so pale and listless that the doctor decided against a return to The Mount. William Cadbury continued to write and Emmie still shared all his letters, which became shorter as he tried to restrain himself; when, as decided by the sisters, no Christmas invitation came from Uffculme she began to feel cut off from all her pleasures; Lucy was to go alone, and surely the excuse that she needed more rest and quiet must have sounded unconvincing. That Christmas, when Emmie was sixteen, William Cadbury wrote to Madagascar and told William and Hannah of all his hopes. He had already waited so long and patiently that he could write:

> I believe others see how much I love her; Jessie, Geraldine, Carrie Senior, and Aunt Elsie give me the truest type of sympathy that is best expressed without words. Edith, Helen and Daisy no doubt talk over (as you suppose) family prospects and draw conclusions . . . Beatrice, I never tried to deceive. Her sweet sisterly sympathy as she

kisses me goodnight proves that she understands. Emmie must not come at Christmas . . . It would not be Emmie who would commit herself, she is quickly developing the tact of her sex . . . I beg you to consider her happiness, you will always be directly adding to mine.

Aunt Hannah also wrote to Madagascar:

Please dear Hannah and Willie pray for me that I may have wisdom to carry out what all feel to be the right thing, without hurting his feelings or any one else's. I say to him and to Emma that my business is to think what is best for Emmie, and he must remember that he has to wait. Theoretically this he is quite willing to do, but when it comes to not seeing her, then he feels it hard, and so it is, but he must bear it.

She was greatly relieved when Emmie's parents agreed with her plans and begged her to keep Emmie at Weston for all her holidays. There is little doubt about their attitude, as Hannah Wilson praised William Cadbury in her letters to Emmie, and continued to tell her that she could always depend on him as a brother for advice and help, and even encouraged her to remember to write to him.

It must have been a relief to everyone when Emmie was pronounced well enough to return to The Mount for the spring term. She was bright and popular and still had her earlier capacity for getting into mischief. Bored by being kept in bed for some minor ailment she warmed up her thermometer on her hot water bottle, and was pleased by the fuss that ensued; years later, when her daughter was at The Mount, the school doctor still remembered her as a 'terror'. He had told her one day that she might have anything she liked to eat; perhaps she had been on his later regime for patients with a temperature, four large glasses of milk, some stone cold, each day; even bread and butter tasted wonderful after that. Emmie immediately asked for pheasant, and always maintained that he sent one for her. It was true that he never forgot her.

During that spring Richard Cadbury and his family set off from Uffculme for a long holiday in Egypt and Palestine. Some years before they had enjoyed one of the earliest camping tours ever organised in the Holy Land, and they were all eager to try further experiments. This time tragedy came to the party; Richard developed diphtheria in Cairo, and died when they reached Jerusalem.

The happy life at Uffculme was sadly darkened, for Emma was deeply attached to her husband and was overwhelmed by his death. By the end of the summer however she remembered a plan made to take 'the little girls' Dorothy Senior, Emmie and Lucy, with Madge Wilson to *Winds Point* on the Malvern Hills.

If William goes with us, she wrote to Hannah [her sister], there will be safety in numbers with all the children together. It will be all right and I shall be with them the whole time. I do not want Emmie to feel that she has done something wrong, or to think that we did not want her at Uffculme; we must be careful . . . as our children will suspect if she is kept away entirely. I will manage things and William is very good.

Emma was doing her best to love and care for the little niece whom she still felt to be childish, empty headed, and inclined to be frivolous. She must have had some comfort in the happiness of all the party. William occupied himself with making a new path up the steep hill to the 'Look out', the summer-house at the top of the garden where they could boil a kettle and make their tea. The days were hot and sunny and Lucy long remembered the fun of tobogganing down the slippery grass slopes of the hills on tea trays. She too was growing up.

Once back at Weston, Aunt Hannah did her best to get Emmie to take life seriously, but after that carefree holiday, with William close at hand, it was hard work. Emmie began to blame her Aunt for some of the restrictions that were being so faithfully carried out on behalf of her parents, and she was conscious of a difference between the Weston household and her Aunt Emma's lavish ways; no visit to Allendale had been allowed that summer, and, knowing nothing of the objection to long bicycle rides, she began to wonder whether there was disapproval of her mother's farming relations. In September her unhappiness and uncertainty burst out in a letter to her mother's sister Lizzie.

> We are beginning in real earnest to get my clothes ready for school [she wrote]. How I wish I was a cat, or at any rate had fur so I need not bother about any. I feel so cross and out of temper because Auntie say's 'you must do this or that', and Hilda says 'you are lazy', but dear Auntie I don't want to grumble, but I do hate to have to be careful and do my own clothes. I don't want to grumble and do not show this letter to anyone, but just tear it up [it was immediately sent to Madagascar]. It is nice to be back home again, though so different from being with the Cadbury's, we have to use our own things and not take any writing paper but our own and so on, but again I say I don't want to grumble but I cannot help feeling the difference very much indeed, we feel as if we were quite separate and almost like orphans, but we ought to be thankful for the mercies God has given and not grumble, but it is such a relief to tell somebody. We had a lovely time at Wynds Point.

How hard it is for children to be part of a home which will never be quite their own, however much they are welcomed there. Emmie could not know the thoughts and and prayers that were behind the disciplines that she resented.

That Autumn Aunt Hannah wrote a long letter to Madagascar.

> You ask about Emmie's progress at school. I think she gets on, but she is certainly backward in many things for her age, music for instance and spelling and arithmetic, but in other things she is quite up to the average, and in English literature and painting I think she does better than most girls. Painting she does better than drawing and has a real taste for it. On the whole she is doing well, her health is strengthening. I was pleased with her report . . . 'Has worked well' comes four times and her diligence is said to be 'very satisfactory' and her general conduct 'very good', so I think we may be well pleased and feel that she is not wasting her time. I think she will be well read for her age and well educated for she takes a lively interest in books, and thinks things out for herself, and has strong youthful opinions of her own which will interest you both greatly. How I wish you could hear her talk; she and Dorothy

discuss all sorts of things together. Physiology, medicine, history, literature, politics, natural history, besides religious matters, and the girls talk with deepest interest, and in this way I learn to know the trend of their thoughts and the influences that are at work in their lives. Emmie is decidedly more of a 'Friend', than she was, which is what you would desire for her. They seem to have discussed 'Friends' versus church when they were at *Winds Point* during the summer in which Helen seems to have led the way and Emmie said after, 'you know Auntie I am a "Friend". I have always avoided comparing Friends doctrine and tried hard to keep to experimental religion in my lessons with them. I could not teach them Friends views, but I abstain from teaching other views, on the points wherein we differ, for I think it is well that in considering her future life, Friends views should be put strongly before her, and that has been done at York and at Doncaster before that. As to the time of her leaving school I scarcely see at present. I enclosed one of William's letters to me in my last letter to you that you might see one sentence in it 'I believe Emmie knows that she is always in my thoughts' I thought it an indication that events might march faster than we anticipate, but if William does not speak and things go on quietly as at present perhaps she might leave school Christmas 12 months; she says she wants to stay at school till she is 18 but it would hardly do for her to be married straight from school, it seems to me now that it might be better for her to leave at 17½ and have singing lessons and a little house keeping work than to stay at York till 1901, but I hold the opinion subject to alteration, and should like to know how things strike you. Perhaps you would not care for William to speak to her till you come, can you tell at present which month you are likely to come home? If you think she ought not to be married till she is 19, then I think it would be well for her to stay at York till July 1901. My medical book says girls should not be married for a year after they have ceased growing, but her father will know all those points. At present Emmie is growing slowly but steadily and is about 5ft 2. I will make a point of measuring her each holidays and let you know. How I wish I could picture her to you, she is much more lively and vivacious than she used to be, is mostly merry and bright, but gets fits of crossness sometimes when things dont go to her mind, and is rather indolent, but there is a softness and charm about her that makes her very attractive, especially to men, both young and old and I must say I admire their taste!! for she is a darling and will delight your hearts . . . I dont quite understand Emma's attitude to Emmie . . . William will never hold out though he is wonderfully self restrained but no one seeing them together could doubt his feelings. I do feel so thankful that she is now over 16 and will be 17 next summer.

After her husband's death Aunt Emma clung to William, as did all her daughters. The two Hannahs agreed that she was talking of Emmie to him because in this way she could keep his interest, but however much she appeared to love Emmie and to welcome the thought of her eventual marriage, they dreaded the possible reaction when the time came to face reality.

Meanwhile Carrie and Richard had been happily married, though Emma could not face the wedding, and the Cadbury sisters attended dressed in deep mourning. Dorothy and Emmie travelled from their respective boarding schools, and the bridesmaids' new frocks looked fresh and dainty among the summer flowers that filled the house. Carrie made a gentle sweet-faced bride in her mother's veil and orange blossoms, and no bridegroom could have enjoyed his wedding more than Richard. Hilda watched her sister feeling that she was indeed so very happy; Richard could hardly keep his eyes off her.

That autumn William Cadbury went away on a long visit to his Cadbury relations in Philadelphia, returning by way of Canada. There was now a valid excuse for letters, and long ones came regularly to Emmie filled with news of his journeys and always including the pressed flowers and ferns which he knew would interest her. He could not help relaxing his self-imposed restraint in other ways and wrote to his dearest Emmie, sending a great deal of love which she seems to have accepted with still innocent gratitude. She wrote openly to Aunt Hannah saying that she really needed a Swan fountain pen for Christmas, because she had such rushes to keep up with an ordinary pen, and she even suggested that Lucy might be encouraged to tell cousin William, should he make enquiries! She also added that she wanted a bicycle basket very much 'but please dont give me a cyclometer, I dreamed last night that you did'.

At school all seemed to be going well that autumn in spite of the lack of a fountain pen. Emmie was head of her class. She was asked to lead a team of girls on the traditional Blackberry Excursion, and they picked the winning weight of blackberries. She had eyes for other things as well and hardly knew how to express her joy. 'There were great tall grasses,' she wrote, 'and gloriously splendidly beautiful seed vessels.'

Alas! when she returned to Weston she found that once again it was Lucy who was invited to Uffculme for Christmas; she was to stay at home to rest after the strenuous term in York. It was harder than ever to believe that her aunt knew what was best, and she was bewildered by the usual excuses. Poor Aunt Hannah must have found it difficult to sound convincing in her assumed anxiety for Emmie's health and the tension was only partly relieved by the arrival of William Cadbury's present, a small mink muff which had come all the way from Montreal. It proved once more that he thought of her and loved her, but why, oh! why, might she not be at Uffculme to thank him herself? It might be added that Aunt Hannah provided the fountain pen.

Since 1897 there had been one recurring question in Aunt Hannah's letters to Madagascar – 'when will you be coming home?' William Wilson's furlough was due in 1900, and it was not too early to think of the time when he and Hannah, with baby Kenneth who had been born in January, would be back in England and able to take up their responsibilities. After much discussion and many letters it was decided that a house should be taken in Weston for that first winter in 1900. They were to leave Madagascar in July, but William had planned to stop in Zanzibar and then visit fellow missionaries in Pemba, leaving Hannah to complete the journey with Kenneth and his nurse. She hoped to reach Marseilles on October 15th.

As the time drew nearer Emmie began to fret over the arrangements for this meeting, so important after six long years of separation. 'Everyone seems to forget that I am your eldest daughter and that I have the right to be the first to meet you' she complained to her mother, desperate lest she should once again be kept at Weston on some flimsy excuse. She must even have felt a little jealous of her dear cousin William, for her mother wrote to beg her to be patient, and to believe that all would be decided for the best, and when she learned that William Cadbury wanted to help in meeting them, she added:

> He will never forget that thou art our eldest daughter Emmie. It is very good of him to offer to come to meet me, and I shall be glad to have him. It was very thoughtful of him to ask if he might come and I am glad that thou said yes, without hesitation. I dont know what we should do without him, he is so thoughtful and good to us, and he has been like a father to thee and Lucy since we left has he not? You can always look up to him as an elder brother, and turn to him for help and counsel.

Her father added his encouragement and word of advice in his letter to this almost unknown daughter:

> . . . by gladly accepting his wish to come and meet us you were giving him great pleasure. It's just one of the little things that we all need to bear in mind. We can't all give each other magnificent and costly presents, it is only rich people who can do that, but we can find out what pleases others, and, even at the cost of a little self denial, do what we know will give them pleasure.

Emmie need have had no fear where her parents sympathy and wishes were concerned, but was she entirely satisfied? William Cadbury took Alec to Paris where they visited the Great Exhibition before meeting all the travellers there, as William Wilson's plans for Zanzibar had wisely been cancelled. Emmie and Lucy were allowed to go by train to Dover where they stayed the night with a Henderson aunt; next day they met the Cross Channel boat, and at last all the planning and waiting was at an end.

The whole family spent the winter together in the lodgings Aunt Hannah had chosen for them in Weston, and in the spring of 1901 they paid a visit to Uffculme. The trees were fresh and

*William Cadbury and Emmie, 1901. Engagement photographs*

green and azalias scented the air as William Cadbury and Emmie walked together in the garden.

She had left The Mount and was to live with her parents in London until they returned to Madagascar when their furlough ended, so for her the future was uncertain. 'I think that I shall train as a nurse', she said, adding a little sadly 'no one seems to want me.' This was more than William could bear, and forgetting his promises he spoke out and set all her fears at rest. It was sometime later when they returned to the house to find everyone gathered round the piano.

Lavender's blue, diddle diddle, lavender's green,
when I am King, diddle diddle, you shall be Queen

they sang, while Emmie looking trustfully up at William knew that for him this was true. She was sure at last of her place in his heart and her home would always be with him.

But there were still to be problems ahead for William and Emmie. Her parents naturally wanted her to be with them for a time, while Aunt Emma, who as a young woman had spent some months in Switzerland learning French and German, felt that Emmie should finish her education, and be given time to grow up in this approved way. So in spite of her protests Emmie was sent to live with a family in Bern, convinced that everyone hoped, and even expected, that William would forget her. It can be imagined how she spent her time in learning a minimal amount of French, exploring Bern with a friend from The Mount who was studying music, day dreaming, and as always, endearing herself to those around her.

Meanwhile William bought the house in Sir Harry's road in Edgbaston which was to be their first home, and wrote long letters to her telling of his plans. There was no danger that he would forget her, but he was so eager to have everything ready for her return that he completely overlooked the fact that she would have liked to take part in the planning. He had always been attracted by the work of living craftsmen, and for the dining room he chose dark oak, with William Morris overtones, made by a well-known designer in Edinburgh; the table was large and heavy enough for a board room. In time it became well suited to a large family, but Emmie never liked it and longed for the elegance of mahogany. She even wrote to her father who tactfully explained her anxieties to William; patterns of materials then began to appear with his letters, and he begged her to tell him her wishes. He must have waited until her return so that she might be with him to choose the white painted furniture for her bedroom, its spacious built-in wardrobes and cupboard, and specially designed panelling and bookcase; with rose coloured curtains at the windows and a deep fender round the fireplace made of soft crimson velvet – this was indeed her own room.

As the long letters flew backwards and forwards William tried to share his wider interests. He, with the other young men of his generation, was deeply involved in Adult School work, but Emmie found it difficult to understand his preoccupation with the troubles of some of the men he met in the Sunday morning classes, though he tried to explain his satisfaction in visiting them, and in finding ways in which he could help them. Emmie would later learn that his self-effacing care for people and his abiding interest in the life of the city would always absorb much of his time and thought. Once with him she began to understand, and as time went on would take her part in the service to the community which was an inherited concern.

How they must have talked together when at last she came

home! Nothing troubled her then. Safe with her father and mother in their new house in London exciting plans for the wedding went forward, and eager to share her joy, she invited cousins and friends to be her bridesmaids, with Lucy as her bridesmaid in chief. There were eight altogether and William would have welcomed eight more if she had asked for them; he wrote in high spirits to congratulate Lucy on being their most important support, with Henry Cadbury as his best man. All went well, and in September of 1902 at the old Quaker Meeting House in Bishopsgate they were married at last!

'They lived happily ever after' – so often the end of the story. This is not the place to write a full account of the fifty-five years William and Emmeline shared together and which fulfilled all William's hopes. The house in Edgbaston, which he prepared with such enthusiasm while Emmie was exiled in Switzerland, became their first home, made radiant by her happiness, and there four children were born, Hannah, John, Alan and Constance. Although less than two miles from the centre of Birmingham they were surrounded by fields and large gardens, but Emmie longed for a country life. When in 1904 a familiar farm on the south of the city was put up for sale, they bought it, building a comparatively small house on the land over which they had walked to Hopwood so long ago. This house became their summer home and there the gardens and plantations were planned and began to take shape. The hill above the house was one of the highest in the district, and appears on an eighth-century document as *Waersetfelda*; in the nineteenth century it was still visited by herb gatherers from Birmingham who came to find the rare Dyer's greenweed and to pick the wild white narcissus that grew on the lower slopes. By then the name had changed to *Wasthull* and later *Hyghe Wastels* and *Wastills*. William chose a modern spelling of the last name for his new house – *Wast Hills*.

Trees were perhaps his first interest, but with Emmeline he chose the roses for the rose beds under the windows and the azalias – a memory of Uffculme. Huge sandstone blocks were brought to make a rockery and to build up the deeper end of the farm pond which had been included in the garden. The holly tree, from which William had once picked a sprig for Emmie's cap, was still growing by the pond and remained there until it was too old to fit in with later improvements. It was he who directed the planting of purple and white crocus round the hedgerow oaks which were left to shade the lawns. For Emmeline there were greenhouses for her carnations and gardenias, and for winter flowers so that vases might be kept filled for every room in the house. She was an unrepentant collector of wild plants, saying in justification that they grew for her. She chose the places they loved round the edge of the pond or in the peat filled bog garden, and each one had an association which made it precious and gave her endless pleasure.

For the first ten years of their married life William was engaged in the investigation of the alleged employment of slaves for growing cocoa in Portuguese West Africa. He made personal visits to Portugal and to the islands of San Thomé and Principe where the cocoa was grown, and was sometimes away for weeks on end. It was a time of great anxiety and strain culminating in a long court case. Emmeline supported him, undaunted by the responsibilities that were her share of the burden. With an able bailiff to oversee the work of the farm and gardens, and with the aid of the first of her devoted secretaries, she undertook the management of two households and the care of her growing family with energy and common sense, and with such success that it was no wonder that the 'little cousin' of Uffculme days began to feel that she could manage anybody. With William's complete love and trust to uphold her and her pride and joy in being his wife, she gathered people round to help her, always eager to give help herself when it was needed.

Emmeline never forgot her school days at The Mount, and was an ardent Old Scholar, telling her children the school stories, and singing school songs. As time went on the pressure of her many good causes was sometimes almost more than she could bear, and in a letter which echoes her Mount days she could wish that a certain demanding enterprise was 'at the bottom of the sea', at the same time involving the whole household in her enthusiasm. Friends could only wonder at her zest for life and all that she achieved.

In 1910 *Wast Hills* was enlarged and became the family home where two more sons, Richard and Brandon, were born.

*Wast Hills, 1907*

*Wast Hills, c.1930*

Remembering her early days in Madagascar pets of all kinds were encouraged, from caterpillars to canaries, from ponies to the peacocks which, with dogs, goats and bantams were her own special interest; she drew the line at cats, but otherwise she just liked seeing animals about as long as somebody else looked after them, and someone always did.

William followed his grandfather John Cadbury in taking a keen interest in local government, becoming a member of the Birmingham City Council in 1911 and Lord Mayor 1919-1921 Emmeline at thirty-six was one of the youngest Lady Mayoresses on record. The Mayoralty coincided with the difficult years which followed the Armistice in 1918. In Birmingham trouble was largely due to unco-ordinated demobilisation. The boom of the war years was followed by depression and strikes, and William had a special concern for the unemployed ex-servicemen. Emmeline was responsible for the organisation of a canteen where they had one meal a day, and during the critical first year, their families were also offered a choice from a variety of substantial foods; she was determined that it should never be a mere soup kitchen. Something of William's devotion to Emmeline and of his reliance on her support comes over in the words of his address on receiving the Freedom of the City in 1938: 'In my public service my truest helper has been my wife. In her presence I cannot tell all that her comradeship and inspiration has meant to me. I also know the place she has in the affection of many in this city'. William was always retiring and found it difficult to get close to those with whom he worked; Emmeline with her impulsive friendliness and her capacity for getting on with all sorts of people supplied the outgoing warmth that made their partnership so successful. A story of the period is worth recording. When Lloyd George the country's wartime Prime Minister came to Birmingham to receive the Freedom of the City, the authorities expected trouble. He had had a rough time some years earlier because of his opposition to the Boer War; this time it was feared that he might be attacked for the part he had played in putting down the Irish rebellion of 1916. As they took their places to process from the Council House to the Town Hall, the Chief Constable said to Emmeline, 'I want you to walk on the crowd side Lady Mayoress; they won't hurt you'.

*Silver Wedding Family Group, 1927*
*(Clockwise from left) John, Richard, Alan, Emmeline, William, Hannah, Constance and Brandon*

After the two years as Lady Mayoress, and with her family rapidly growing up, she had more time for other commitments, notably with the Birmingham Girl Guides and the National Council of Women, and she later became a magistrate, but her home and family were always the centre of her life and, remembering her own childhood, she welcomed and befriended a number of boys and girls who for the time being had no settled home. Her youngest brother Kenneth for whom she had special care wrote at her death that *Wast Hills* had been the one constant factor in his life, and this was true for his sons; others, whose work took them about the world, knew that a welcome was always waiting for them when they came home to England.

William returned to his work at Bournville, and together they undertook the long sea journey to Tasmania where for two months they watched the establishment of the Cadbury Factory there, Emmeline as much needed as ever for making friends, and supporting and encouraging the wives who had followed their husbands to help with the founding of this new venture. With William she visited Ghana (then the Gold Coast) and the West Indies, but she was no natural traveller, content with long

*Emmeline, County Commissioner, 1938*

summer fishing holidays in Ireland or Scotland with the family, which were the pattern for some years in the twenty's and early thirty's.

William and Emmeline were members of Bull Street Meeting and they warmly supported Quaker activities, Emmeline journeying to Yearly Meeting in London, and both having a special interest in overseas work, as well as in the missionary college of Kingsmead in Birmingham. Emmeline's faith with its theme of love and service was reflected in a book of favourite quotations and texts which she collected for her children. For many years she was president of a large womens' group which met each Monday, and which, besides providing a simple service with Bible readings and much cheerful hymn singing, supplied organised help for its members at a time when there was no welfare state or health service. With her own children so close to her heart Emmeline cared deeply for the women and their problems, and they never forgot the weekly talks drawn from her personal belief and experience. At these meetings she herself learnt much, developing great spiritual force of character, which in her wider work for the city enabled her to calm meetings which everyone expected to be stormy, and which was remembered as a very real inspiration. This simple practical faith was recognised wherever she went, and it was a member of the National Council of Women who felt that she was an almost perfect example of a good woman.

When William became severely crippled with arthritis, and for the last years was bedridden, he encouraged her many trips to London for committees, saying that they made life so much more interesting for him, though he became fearful of accidents if she did not return when expected.

These days in London gave her a much needed break from the problems of her household, and she delighted in the gasps of astonishment from porters and passengers when she arrived at Euston Station carrying an overflowing basket of flowers, particularly when they were the vivid blue autumn gentians, which were so carefully tended in her garden, and which were always gifts for special occasions.

William died in 1957 and life for Emmeline was never the same again; during the nine years without him some of the uncertanties and anxieties of her early years seemed to return, and she was bewildered by social changes which she could not understand.

She lost much of her old energy, but still kept the independence which reached out to a wide circle of friends and relations. Her home was the centre of the family where children and grandchildren were lovingly welcomed, finding at *Wast Hills* the stability of a vanishing way of life that warmed and refreshed them. Great-grandchildren came in their carry-cots, to be introduced and blessed; grandchildren felt welcome for themselves, a small room next to the old nursery being ready if they came to stay with her. She would listen to their adventures

*William and Emmeline, 1939*

and problems, so different from those of her own youth, then she would bring out the treasures which she had collected over many years, and which all had stories of their own. Like her grandmother, Hannah Henderson, she sat upright in her chair, her hands often busy with the knitting and cross-stitch that helped to fill her quiet hours. When a guest was leaving she would find something to give them, perhaps gathering up an armful of scented carnations from the vase on her own table for a friend who had no garden. Grandchildren who came to say goodbye before returning to boarding school would be taken to a certain cupboard where she kept the sweet things that she never ate herself. 'I don't think you would like this' she would say, contemplating a box of chocolates before returning it to its shelf, yet always, in the end, finding a generous supply to cheer their wilting spirits.

On Christmas day all who could make the journey came to *Wast Hills* to gather round her Christmas tree, which in memory of the snow-covered firs of Switzerland was always trimmed in sparkling white and silver. There they sang the old carols, and thought of the Christmas story which she loved so much. Then came the ritual distribution of the presents all carefully chosen and wrapped, and piled beneath the branches. From the youngest to the oldest everyone took turns to pick up a parcel and give it to its owner. This was the crowning moment of her year as she sat surrounded by her family, happy in watching each one and enjoying them all, while above them the soft light of the candles twinkled on the trembling tinsel of the tree.

*A Victorian Candle Holder from Emmeline's Tree*

Emmeline died peacefully on a summer night in 1966. She had been staying in the Lake District, a favourite place for holidays after William's death; that year the long drive back to *Wast Hills* had been particularly trying and she was glad to be at home again. She had planned to hold three garden parties soon after her return, and there was not much time for the rest she needed, but by the end of a week she was ready to entertain her guests, and took her usual part in directing the preparations. She much looked forward to welcoming a group of retired nurses, for whom she had helped to found a Trust when she was Lady Mayoress. The day before their visit was cold and showery, and she was troubled about the mats which covered the wet grass in the tea tent; impulsive as ever, she had even tried to rearrange them herself.

Next day, June 25th, brought warmth and sunshine and she was at her best in the home she loved so much, talking to her old friends and enjoying the garden with them. In the evening she suffered a severe stroke and never regained consciousness, but she had, on that last day, been able to pass on something of the happiness that had blessed her so generously during the long years shared with William – years of experience and opportunity for which she never ceased to be thankful.

*Emmeline Hannah Cadbury, a portrait by Charles M. Gere, 1918*

# Bibliography

*Richard Cadbury*
by Helen Cadbury Alexander
(Hodder and Stoughton, London, 1906)

*William A. Cadbury*
printed for private circulation, 1958

*Family papers*

*Friends in Madagascar 1867-1967*
by Winifred White (Friends Service Council)

*A Man in Shining Armour*
by A. J. and G. Gosfield (Headley Bros, 1911)

*The Martys Isle*
by Annie Sharman (The London Missionary Society, 1909)

*List of Teachers and Scholars, The Mount School*
1784-1814: 1831-1906 (William Sessions, York, 1906)

*A History of Wigton School 1815-1915*
(Wigton Old Scholars Association 1916)

# Index

ACKWORTH School, 17
  *Flounders Institute*, 17
Allendale, Rector of, 4
Allendale, relations, x
Ambahimanga, *old capital*
  *Madagascar*, 36
Amboniriana, 45, 47
Antananarivo (Tanarive), 18, 20, 27-8
  *English Hospital*, 26, 33, 35, 37, 41
  *French attack*, 35-8
  *Infectious Hospital*, 35-6
  *Lady Superintendent of Hospital*,
    Miss Byam, 36-7
  *Medical Supervisor*, Dr.
    Ramorasata, 40
  *Mission House*, 57
Arivonimamo, 40, 43, 47
  *Friends Mission*, 38

BARCLAYS *Apology*, 2
Bigland, Percy, *Quaker artist*, 12
Bradley, Mr., *visitor*, 37

CADBURY, Emma J. (neé Wilson),
  sister to William Wilson, 17, 33,
  35, 45, 64-5, 73-4, 84
  m. Richard Cadbury, *as second wife*
  Parents: John Ashlin Wilson and
    Emma Smith
  Daus: Edith, 64, 73, 75-6, 79;
    (*m*. Arnold Butler, 75, 77);
    Helen, 33, 64, 73, 76-7, 84;
    Margaret (Daisy), 33, 64, 73,
    76-7, 79, 84; Beatrice, 33, 64,
    76, 79
  *Step-dau:* Jessie, 73, 79
  *Step-sons:* Barrow, 64, 77
    (*m*. Geraldine Southall, 79);
    William Adlington, *see* W. A.
    Cadbury; Richard, 64, 75, 84
    (*m*. Caroline Senior)
  *Christmas Visits*, 64-6, 73, 75, 77
  *Holiday in Egypt and Palestine*, 80

  *Homes:* Uffculme, 73, 75; Winds
    Point, 69, 81-3
  *Husband's death:* 81, 84
  *Nurse:* Emma Denham, 33
**Cadbury, Emmeline (Emmie)**
  **Hannah (neé Wilson),**
  **3rd Hannah;**
  *m*. William Adlington Cadbury
  Parents: William Wilson and
    Hannah Henderson
  Siblings: *see* Hannah Wilson's
    children
  Children: Hannah Henderson
    (Joy), John, Alan, Constance,
    Richard, Brandon, 60, 89, 95
  *Grandchildren:* 95
  *Gt. grandchildren:* 95
  *Grandmother:* **Hannah I**, 67, 96
  *Gt. grandmother:* Mary Hall, 67
  Cousins: Madge Wilson, 79, 81;
    Willie Wilson, 79
  *Allendale*, 5, 63-4, 67, 69, 73, 78
  *Birth and babyhood*, 21, 58
  *Birthday gifts*, 64
  *Blackford*, 31, 66-70, 73
  *Carrying chairs (palanquins)*, 22, 62
  *Deaths of siblings: see* Hannah
    Wilson
  *Doncaster*, 68
  *Dress allowance*, 70
  *Elsie, ring of Aunt* (wife of George
    Cadbury), 64
  *English relations*, 64
  *Excursions*, 62
  *Furlough*, 63
  *Further education* (Bern), 87
  *Girl Guide Commissioner*, 94
  *Growing up*, 56, 59
  *Homes:* 60, 62, 85; Edgbaston,
    88-9; Wast Hills, 89-91; Wast
    Hills holly tree, 74, 89
  *Husband's death*, 95
  *Illness*, 78
  *Lady Mayoress*, 92-3, 98
  *Left in England*, 66-8

101

*Letters to parents*, 69
*Letter to Aunt Lizzie* (Elizabeth Henderson), 81-2
*Magistrate*, 93
*Mandridrano, journey to*, 60
*National Council of Women*, 93
*Nurse, Neney*, 21, 47, 57, 62
*Parcels, arrival of*, 57-60
*Parents return to England*, 85-6
*Party dress*, 58
*Ravanalona III's brooch*, 50-1
*Reward for sewing Charlie's shirts*, 71
*Schooldays*, 48, 66, 71-2, 74, 76, 78, 80, 82-3
*Senior, Caroline, wedding of*, 84
*Smallpox*, 25
*Society of Friends, membership of*, 83
*Sunday evenings in Madagascar*, 63
*Uffculme, Christmas at*, 64-5, 73, 75, 77, 79, 80, 85-6
*Weston-Super-Mare, journey to*, 78
*William*: Christmas gift from, 85; engagement to, 87; feelings for, 77, 79; marriage to, 49; plans for marriage, 83, 88; wedding, 88
*Winds Point*, 69, 81-3
*Women's Group, weekly*, 94-5
*Visits*: Algeria and Marseilles, 49, 51; Ghana, Tasmania and West Indies, 93
*Death*, 95

**Cadbury, Hannah Henderson, 4th Hannah**; *see* Taylor

Cadbury, Richard, 30, 64, 70, 75
   *m.* (1) Elizabeth Adlington
   *children: see* Emma J. Cadbury
   *m.* (2) Emma J. Wilson
   *children: see* Emma J. Cadbury
   *Death*, 80
Cadbury, William Adlington
   *Parents:* Richard Cadbury and Elizabeth Adlington
   *Grandfather:* John Cadbury
   *Siblings: see* Emma J. Cadbury (step-mother)
   *Step-siblings: see* Emma J. Cadbury (step-mother)
   **m. Emmeline Hannah Wilson, 3rd Hannah**, 49
   *Children: see* Emmeline Hannah Cadbury
   *1st cousin:* Henry Cadbury (Best man at wedding), 89
   *Batchelor activities*, 74, 77
   *Adult School work*, 88
   *Emmie*, feelings for, 47, 74, 76-80; first meeting, 17; marriage, 49; The Mount School fees, 74
   *Letters*, 47, 73, 84
   *Local Government*, 92
   *Lord Mayor*, 92
   *Senior, Hannah, help to*, 70
   *Slavery investigation*, 90
   *Support to William Wilson*, 73
   *Visits*: Algeria, 49; Cadbury factory, Tasmania, 93; Marseilles, 49, 95; Philadelphia, 84
   *Death*, 95
Carroll, Mary, x, 50; Will, 50
Charles, Prince, 1
Clark, Henry, 68
   *m.* —— (Dadabe), 68
Clark, Joseph Firth, 33, 68, 69
   *Dau:* Nannie, 33, 64, 69, 71
   *Sons:* Oswald, 68; Bernard, 68

Fox, George, 1
*George Fox's Journal*, 2
French: *Invasion*, 35, 38; *Navy*, 20; *Resident*, General Gallibéni, 42, 44, General Laroche, 41; *wife*, Madame Laroche, 41; *rule*, 41-2
Friends Foreign Mission Association, 48-9, 63-4; *secretary*, Watson, Grace, 48
Friends Syrian Mission, Brummana, 48

GILPIN, Helen, *Headmistress*, 61
Graham, John, 2, 4, 67
   *son* Geordie, 67
Gretna Green, 4, 67

Grey, Sir Edward, 35
**HALL, Hannah, 1st Hannah,** *see* Henderson
  *m*. Matthew Henderson
  *Parents:* Isaac Hall and Mary Philipson
Hall, Isaac I, (17th c.), 1, 2
Hall, Isaac II, 1-4, 6-8, 67
  *Parents*, 2-3, 8;
  *Sisters*, 2, 4; Sarah, 2-5, 8
  *Brother*, 2
  *m*. Mary Philipson, 1-8, 14, 67
  *Buried*, 11
  *Children*, 4, 7-8
  *Death of wife*, 8
  *Wedding certificate*, 6
Hall, Mad Jack, 1
**Henderson, Hannah (neé Hall), 1st Hannah,** x, 1, 7-8, 15, 28-9
  *m*. Matthew Henderson, 1, 8-9, 11-12, 15-16, 29, 67
  *Children:* Sarah, Mary, 9; twins Matthew and Robert, 9, 15; Lizzie, 9, 31, 54; Fanny, Amy and Maggie, 9, 11
  *Grandchildren:* Alec and Mary Wilson, 10
  *Grandmother Shield*, 1, 12
  *Siblings*, 7; Jane, 8; John, 8; Susannah, 8
  *Education*, 8
  *Helpful daughter*, 7
  *Homes:* Glenholme, 9; The Hope, 9, 29, 32, 54, 67; Keenley Side Hill, 9, 16; Wham Lands, 9, 15-6
  *Old age*, 12
  *Portrait*, 12
  *Riding to Meeting*, 16
  *Visit from Hannahs III and IV*, x, xi
  *Death and Burial*, 12
Henderson, John (friend of Hannah II), 16
Henderson, Matthew (*see* Hannah Henderson)
Hexham Prison, 1
*High Studdon*, 2, 3, 7

Hova tribe, Madagascar, 20, 36

*ISOAVINA* (holiday home), 28
Itasy, lake, 44, 61

JESUITS, 43

KINGSMEAD Missionary College, 52, 94
Kylie cow, 10

LONDON Missionary Society, 21, 27
Dr. Fenn, 27, 35

MANDRIDRANO, district of, 22, 24-29, 38-40, 43, 45, 60-1, 63
  *English Hospital*, 26, 40-1
  *Medical Supervisor*,
    Dr. Ramorasata, 40
  *Mission Hospital*, 62
Meeting Houses: Allendale, 4, 5, 8, 12, 67; Allendale Burial Ground, 12, 54; Berwick, 2; Bull Street, Birmingham, 94; Devonshire House, 49, 89; Doncaster, 68; Hexham, 2; Hitchin, 49; Newcastle, 2
Missionaries in Madagascar: Clark, Mr., 35, 38; Herbert, Clara, 19, 37, 42, 44, 50-1; Johnson, William, 28, 38-40; Johnson, Lucy, 38-40; *Dau:* Blossom, 38, 40; Robson, Ernest, 40; Standing, Mr. and Mrs., 40
Missionary Helpers Union, England, 44
Mountmellick School, 52
Mount School, York, The, 18, 44, 48, 71, 74-8, 80, 82-3, 85, 87, 90

PHILIPSON, Mary, *see* Isaac Hall II
  *Parents:* Francis Philipson, and Mary Green (previously married to — Nattress)
Protestant Churches, 21; Missions, 41, 43

QUEENS of Madagascar: *Ranavalona I*, xi, 17; *Ranavalona III*, 26, 34-5, 41-2, 49-51, 62
*Abdication*, 42
*Aunt*, Princess Ramasindrazaney, 42, 49, 51
*Brooch*, xi, 50-1
*Crown*, xi, 42
*1st husband*, 50
*2nd husband*, 50
*Palace*, 35-6, 42

RELIGIOUS Society of Friends, 21
Roberts, Mrs. (Winchmore Hill friend), 52

SACLAVA Tribe, 62
Senior, Hannah (neé Wilson)
 *m*. Charles Senior, the Rev., 31, 48, 66
 *Parents*: John Ashlin Wilson and Emma Smith, 70, 75
 *Dau*: Dorothy, 31, 33, 66-7, 69, 73, 75, 79, 81-2, 84
 *Son*: Charles, 33, 66-7, 71
 *Step-daus*: Caroline (Carry), 66-7, 75, 78-9, 84; Hilda, 66-7, 70-1, 74, 82, 84
 *Step-son*: Arthur, 66-7, 70, 79
 *Aunt, elderly*, 70
 *Caroline's wedding*, 84
 *Ill-health*, 33, 78
 *Letters from Emmie*, 76
 *Letters to Emmie's parents*, 69, 74, 80-4
 *The Mount uniform for Emmie*, 74
Shield family, 12
Shield, grandmother of Hannah Hall, 1, 12
Slavery, 24-5, 34
Slavery, *abolition of*, 42
Society for the Propogation of the Gospel, 35, 41

TAYLOR, Christopher B.
 *m*. Hannah Henderson Cadbury (4th Hannah)

**Taylor, Hannah Henderson** (neé Cadbury), **4th Hannah,** x, xi, 80, 89
 *m*. Christopher B. Taylor
 *Parents*: William A. and **Emmeline Hannah Cadbury 3rd Hannah**
 *Brothers*: John, Alan, Richard, Brandon, 93
 *Sister*: Constance, 93
 *Grandparents*: William and **Hannah Wilson, 2nd Hannah**
 *Gt. grandparents*: Matthew and **Hannah Henderson, 1st Hannah**
 *Children*: Elizabeth, Arthur & James (twins), Clare, Mary

VICTORIA, Queen, death of, 48

WILSON, **Hannah** (neé Henderson), **2nd Hannah**
 *m*. William Wilson
 *Parents*: Matthew and **Hannah Henderson, 1st Hannah**
 *Siblings: see* Hannah Henderson's children
 *Children: see* **Emmeline H. Cadbury**; John Ashlin, 22, 58; Lucy Mary, 10, 22, 24-6, 28-9, 32-3, 38, 44, 47-9, 51, 61-2, 66-7, 69-70, 73, 75, 78-9, 81, 85-6, 89; Wm. Alexander (Alec), x, 10, 28-9, 33, 47, 52, 67, 73-5, 86; Samuel Basil, 32-4, 67; Robert Kenneth, 45-7, 51-2, 85, 89
 *Grandchildren*, 52, 64
 *Birth*, 9
 *Youth*, 16
 *Classes*, 34, 43-4, 47
 *Death*, 54
 *Deaths of children*: Ashlin, 21-2, 58; Basil, 33, 68
 *Education*: Wigton, 17; The Mount, *see* The Mount School
 *French attacks and rule*: 20, 41-2
 *Furlough*, 28-9, 85

*Homes:* Birmingham, 52; Gerards Cross, 54; Glenholme, 54; Hitchin, 49; Weston-Super-Mare, 48, 80; Winchmore Hill, 48
*Home letters and parcels,* 24, 28, 35-40, 47, 57, 78-80
*Illnesses,* 26-7, 33, 49
*Johnson tragedy,* 38-40
*Leaving children in England,* 33, 66
*Madagascar,* arrival 18-20; first years, 24-8; riots, 35-8; servants, 24, 27, 34, 37, 57, 61-2; slaves (Ratasy, 24), 24-5, 34; pets, 61; visits to Mandridrano, 44; visit to Madeira, 43
*Ranavalona, Queen, brooch of,* 50-1
*School,* 44
*Visits:* Algeria, 49; Canada, 52; Egypt and Palestine, 48; Marseilles, 49
Wilson, William
  *m.* Hannah Henderson, 19
  *Parents:* John Ashlin Wilson and Emma Smith, 27-8, 40
  *Sisters:* Emma Cadbury, Hannah Senior

*Children, see* Hannah Wilson
*Death,* 51
*Education and training,* 17-18, 25, 30, 32, 66
*Joined Friends,* 17
*British Committee of Safety,* 35
*Friends Foreign Mission Association (F.F.M.A.),* 49
*Furlough,* 18, 28-9, 48, 85
*Homes,* 20, 22, 33-4, 45, 48, 63, 85
*Illness,* 51, 61
*Letters and parcels from home,* 28, 45, 47, 57-8, 69-70, 73, 77, 80, 82, 85
*Madagascar:* First years, 17-20, 24-8; Hospital work, 25-6, 44, 62; Johnson tragedy, 38-40; Naturalist, 61; Pony *Merrylegs,* 39; Private practice, 41; Riots, 39-41
*Smallpox,* 25, 44
*Visits;* Ceylon, 49; China, 49; Egypt and Palestine, 48; India, 49; Pemba, 85; Zanzibar, 86
Wigton School, 8, 17
World War II, 52

## Chart I  THE THREE HANNAHS

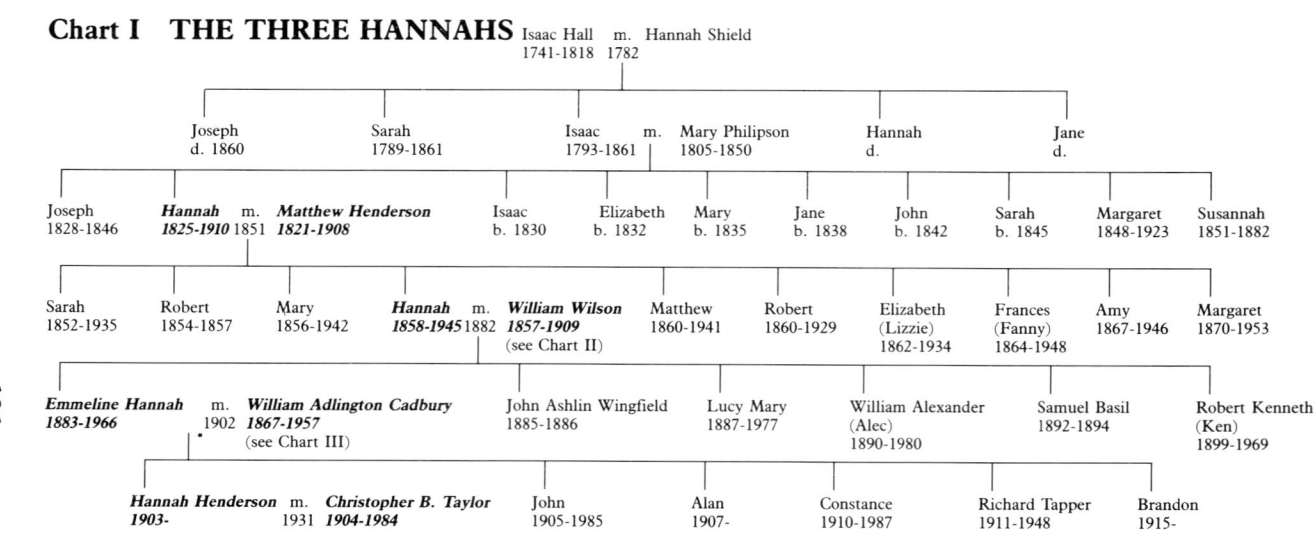

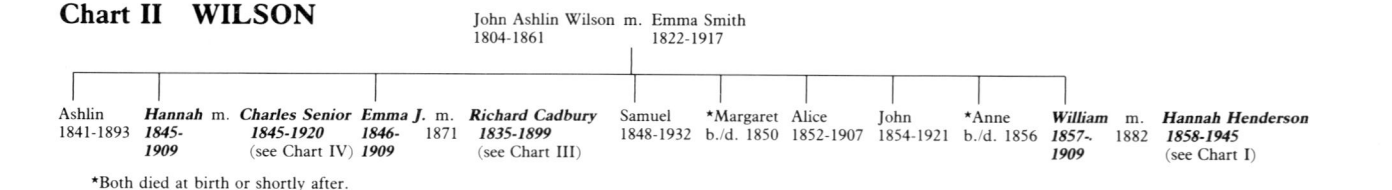

Isaac Hall  m.  Hannah Shield
1741-1818  1782

Descendants:

- Joseph d. 1860
- Sarah 1789-1861
  - Joseph 1828-1846
  - **Hannah** *1825-1910* 1851 m. **Matthew Henderson** *1821-1908*
    - Sarah 1852-1935
    - Robert 1854-1857
    - Mary 1856-1942
    - **Hannah** *1858-1945* 1882 m. **William Wilson** *1857-1909* (see Chart II)
      - *Emmeline Hannah* 1883-1966 m. **William Adlington Cadbury** 1902 *1867-1957* (see Chart III)
      - *Hannah Henderson* 1903- m. **Christopher B. Taylor** 1931 *1904-1984*
    - John Ashlin Wingfield 1885-1886
    - Lucy Mary 1887-1977
      - John 1905-1985
      - Alan 1907-
      - Constance 1910-1987
    - William Alexander (Alec) 1890-1980
    - Samuel Basil 1892-1894
    - Richard Tapper 1911-1948
      - Brandon 1915-
    - Robert Kenneth (Ken) 1899-1969
- Isaac 1793-1861 m. Mary Philipson 1805-1850
  - Isaac b. 1830
  - Mary b. 1835
  - Jane b. 1838
  - Elizabeth b. 1832
  - Matthew 1860-1941
  - Robert 1860-1929
  - John b. 1842
  - Elizabeth (Lizzie) 1862-1934
  - Frances (Fanny) 1864-1948
  - Sarah b. 1845
  - Margaret 1848-1923
  - Amy 1867-1946
  - Susannah 1851-1882
  - Margaret 1870-1953
- Hannah d.
- Jane d.

## Chart II  WILSON

John Ashlin Wilson  m.  Emma Smith
1804-1861      1822-1917

- Ashlin 1841-1893
- **Hannah** *1845-1909* m. **Charles Senior** *1845-1920* 1871 (see Chart IV)
- Emma J. 1846-1909
- *Margaret b./d. 1850
- Alice 1852-1907
- John 1854-1921
- *Anne b./d. 1856
- **William** *1857-1909* m. 1882 **Hannah Henderson** *1858-1945* (see Chart I)
- Samuel 1848-1932
- **Richard Cadbury** *1835-1899* (see Chart III)

*Both died at birth or shortly after.

## Chart III  CADBURY

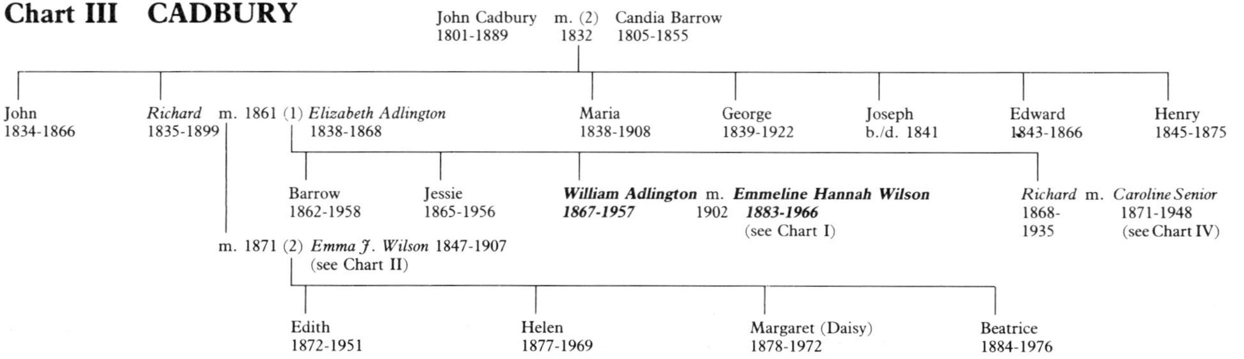

John Cadbury  m. (2)  Candia Barrow
1801-1889      1832    1805-1855

Children:
- John 1834-1866
- Richard 1835-1899  m. 1861 (1) Elizabeth Adlington 1838-1868; m. 1871 (2) Emma J. Wilson 1847-1907 (see Chart II)
- Maria 1838-1908
- George 1839-1922  m. Emmeline Hannah Wilson 1883-1966 (see Chart I), William Adlington 1867-1957, m. 1902
- Joseph b./d. 1841
- Edward 1843-1866
- Henry 1845-1875

Children of Richard and Elizabeth Adlington:
- Barrow 1862-1958
- Jessie 1865-1956

Children of Richard and Emma J. Wilson:
- Edith 1872-1951
- Helen 1877-1969
- Margaret (Daisy) 1878-1972
- Beatrice 1884-1976
- Richard 1868-1935  m. Caroline Senior 1871-1948 (see Chart IV)

## Chart IV  SENIOR

Rev. Charles J. Senior  m. (1) Caroline Fry 1845-1872
1845-1920              m. (2) Hannah Wilson 1845-1909 (see Chart II)

Children:
- Arthur 1868-1947
- Edith 1869-1950
- Caroline 1871-1948  m. Richard Cadbury 1868-1935 (see Chart III)
- Hilda 1872-1956
- Charles A. L. 1877-1938
- H. Dorothea (Dorothy) 1884-1953

107

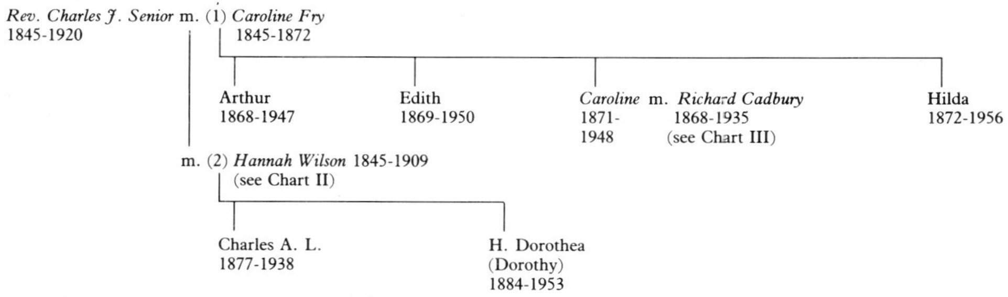